MAIL PILOT LINE

WAY BILL,

FROM

Philadelphia to Wheeling.

June 10ᵗ 183_

Arrival   Chamber g.   Departure

1. 15   2. 36

TRAIN WRECKS

TRAIN WRECKS

*A Pictorial History
of Accidents on
The Main Line*

By Robert C. Reed

BONANZA BOOKS · NEW YORK

This edition is published by Bonanza Books, distributed by Crown Publishers, Inc., 225 Park Avenue South, New York, New York 10003, by arrangement with Darwin Publications, Inc.

Manufactured in the United States of America

Library of Congress Cataloging in Publication Data

Reed, Robert Carroll, 1937–
    Train wrecks.

    Reprint. Originally published: 1st ed. Seattle:
Superior Pub. Co., 1968.
    Bibliography: p.
    1. Railroads—United States—Accidents—History.
I. Title.
[HE1780.R4   1982]   363.1'22'0973   82-14574
ISBN: 0-517-328976

    w   v   u   t   s

This book is dedicated to locomotive engineer William Henry Talbott, great-grandfather of the author, who lost his life in the line of duty on February 27, 1865, at Crestline, Ohio, serving the Cleveland, Columbus & Cincinnati Railroad.

CONTENTS

FOREWORD

I feel particularly close to the subject of this book, having survived a frightening rail derailment in the wilds of West Virginia, in which my coach toppled off the rails, turned over, and slid on its side for several hundred feet. But personal experience is no prerequisite for reading this book. Mr. Reed has prepared a concise history of American railroad accidents, which is embellished with enough contemporary accounts to give the reader a feeling of the times. He has also assembled a remarkable collection of photographs and engravings to illustrate the more important types of accidents.

The railway as the first means of mechanical transportation ushered in an era of fast and comparatively comfortable travel. At first the public seemed ready to accept the dangers inherent in this new technology, but eventually many of the difficulties and dangers were corrected by experience gained from a decade or two of trial and error. Some problems were never completely solved, of course, and train wrecks continued to plague the traveller despite the great engineering advancements made during the last half of the nineteenth century.

Although accidents began with the first railroad operations in this country, the early years were generally free from serious disasters. Light traffic and slow speeds account for this good early safety record. By mid-century, however, the enormous growth of the rail network and the corresponding growth in traffic together with the introduction of nighttime travel reduced the margin of safety considerably. Primitive signaling systems, laminated iron rails, and brittle cast iron wheels contributed their hazards to railroading in this country. But as always human error was the main cause of accidents. It might be suggested here that the public outcry against the dangers of rail travel took a vengeful personal note compared to the fatalistic acceptance of road and sea disasters that were somehow considered as natural calamities.

Late in the nineteenth century a number of important technical inventions combined to improve the safety of rail travel. Cheap steel brought sound rails, axles, and bridges. Automatic electric signals, double track, and the Westinghouse brake made their contributions. The fire hazard was banished by the adoption of electric lighting and steam heating about the turn of the century. All of these efforts were culminated by the adoption of the all steel passenger car in 1907. Today railroads are the safest mode of travel available to Americans.

JOHN H. WHITE
Former Curator of Transportation
United States National Museum
Smithsonian Institution

MAIL PILOT LINE

WAY BILL,

FROM

Philadelphia to Wheeling.

June 10th 183

Arrival Charles G. Departure

1·15   2.36

TRAIN WRECKS

This antique engraving from Howland's **STEAMBOAT DISASTERS AND RAILROAD ACCIDENTS,** published in 1840, shows the first head-on collision that caused the death of railroad passengers. The accident happened on the Portsmouth & Roanoke Railroad (now the Seaboard) near Suffolk, Virginia, on August 11, 1837. An eastbound lumber train running fast (for those days) on a down grade, lurched around a sharp curve and ran furiously into the morning passenger train from Portsmouth. Aboard the thirteen stagecoach-like coaches were 200 Virginians returning to their homes from a steamboat cruise. The first three coaches were crushed to pieces in the concussion. Killed in the havoc were three young ladies of the prominent Ely family, and a dozen others were brutally maimed. Blame for the calamity was put on the willful mismanagement and gross negligence of the captain and engineer of the lumber train.

A. Jaynes, Pr., Pittsburgh, Pa

Chapter One

Early Railroad Accidents

RAILROADS IN AMERICA were remarkably free from serious accidents during the first twenty years or so of their operation. From 1829 until 1853 there weren't any really disastrous wrecks. Although a few passengers were killed in the early days, the number of fatalities was few compared to the time after the Civil War when the death rate from railroad wrecks went up alarmingly. Up until 1853 no more than half a dozen people were killed in any single wreck. On May 6, 1853, however, the early safety record of railroading in America came to a sudden halt; on that day forty-six people were killed in a head-on collision at Secaucus, New Jersey.

There are a number of explanations for the early safety of railroads during the 1830's and 1840's. For one thing railroad operations were rather primitive. Trains ran slowly in those days, seldom faster than ten to eighteen miles an hour. The tracks were simply too poor to allow trains to go very fast. Also, because of the relatively light traffic then, there were not many trains in operation. There was scarcely any night travel until after 1850. When a rare passenger train was run after dark, it was usually preceded by a pilot engine which led the way over the twisting, bumpy track to discover whether or not the right-of-way ahead was clear and safe. Broken rails, faulty switches, and washed out bridges were an ever present danger. If there was a hazard on the track, the pilot engine, not the passenger train, was involved.

Runs in the early days were short. The track mileage for the entire country in 1835 was only 1,098 miles. Even by 1850 after twenty years of railroad expansion only 9,021 miles of track had been laid. Consequently, with the short trips and low density of traffic, railroad travel remained fairly safe in spite of primitive operations.

Wrecks did happen, of course. Cows wandered on the track, or a rail snapped causing a derailment; such occurrences were numerous. Still, in spite of the frequency of such mishaps, few lives were lost. Because of the slow speeds trains traveled, a collision or a derailment did not cause a catastrophe. Even a collision between two trains running in opposite directions did not produce a disaster during the first two decades of railroad operation. Passenger cars were so light and flimsy in those years that the impact of a collision was slight.

On March 2, 1836, a head-on collision on the Camden & Amboy, a pioneer road which ran from Philadelphia to New York City across the New Jersey fields, caused a terrific smash up, but nobody was injured. In fact the passengers appeared rather cavalier about the wreck. In a dense coastal fog a passenger train and a freight train hauling lumber crashed head-on near Burlington, New Jersey. According to an eye witness, the engines mounted up "like two dogs in a fight. The engineers and firemen sprang off at the moment of the concussion and saved themselves. The passengers were electrified, and a bruise here and there betokened that a shock of no slight nature had occurred. The locomotives were broken into many pieces. Breast to breast, they seemed to be in deadly strife." The passengers seemed to take the collision in their stride, for we are told that, "some of the passengers footed it to Burlington; others were brought in sleighs; some remained at a farm house hard by; whilst others lingered about the ruins." Before long another train was sent to the scene and took them on their way to Camden." No one seems to have been terribly distressed by the acci-

dent. They simply viewed the wreck as a delay or an annoyance to put up with in railroad travel.

The first word used in America to describe a railroad collision, *concussion,* describes the jarring, jolting nature of early collisions when passengers were thrown about rather roughly but seldom killed.

The first person to be killed in an American railroad was on the South Carolina Road when the company's pioneer locomotive *The Best Friend of Charleston* exploded and killed the engine fireman, a Negro slave. The explosion, which happened on June 17, 1831, was caused when the fireman became annoyed by the loud hissing noise of steam escaping from the safety valve. To stop the noise, he simply held the valve down. The boiler promptly burst, sending the slave aflying. At the time of this accident the South Carolina Road, running from Charleston to Hamburg for 135 miles, was the longest railroad in the world. Also, the *Best Friend* was the first locomotive built in the United States for commercial use.

THESE TWO VERMONT CENTRAL LOCOMOTIVES were caught by an amateur photographer after they came to rest, one atop the other, in May 1864.

THE F. B. SMITH proved to be just too heavy for the wooden bridge at Birkfield, Mass. The accident occurred on the Portland and Oxford Central line in the 1860's.

Although the explosion of the *Best Friend* is an historical "first," it was actually not an accident but rather a mechanical failure; also its victim was an employee rather than a passenger. The first accident to kill a passenger happened on the Camden & Amboy. This accident, near Hightstown, New Jersey, on November 11, 1833, was caused by a broken axle on one of the cars. The train was going twenty-five miles an hour, a high speed for the time, when the axle snapped. The cars were immediately derailed, and the wooden coaches upset and smashed apart. A number of passengers were thrown about, bruised, and banged up. One man, Mr. James C. Stedman, a jeweler from Raleigh, North Carolina, was so badly injured that he died within a few hours, thus becoming the country's first railroad passenger fatality. Another passenger on the train, though uninjured, was ex-president John Quincy Adams.

This derailment on the Camden & Amboy is significant in American railroad history in a far more important way than simply killing the first passenger on record. It was a passenger who was not killed in this wreck who was later to shape railroad history. The passenger was Cornelius "Commodore" Vanderbilt. When the axle on the car ahead of the Commodore's broke, Vanderbilt's own car overturned. Vanderbilt was pitched out of the car and flung down a thirty-foot embankment; one of his lungs was punctured, and several of his ribs were broken. He was taken to his home in New York and there hovered between life and death for a month.

Largely because of his injuries from this accident, Vanderbilt refused to invest any of his immense fortune in railroads. He had always distrusted what he called the "new-fangled" railroads, and his distrust turned to outright hatred after his first train ride which nearly killed him. Oddly enough, in spite of his early hatred of railroads, Vanderbilt was to become the greatest of the railroad barons. At the ripe old age of sixty-eight, with an $11,-

11

THE EASTERN RAILROAD'S 72 took care not to mar her handsome looks when she slid down the bank at Newburyport, Mass.

THE AFTERMATH OF A HEAD-ON COLLISION on the Albany Northern Railroad circa 1860. Much of the wreckage has already been piled on the flat cars in the foreground.

000,000 fortune made from steamboats, the Commodore turned to railroads in 1862. Before he died in 1877 he controlled the vast New York Central system.

Since few people were killed in accidents during the first twenty years of railroading, the American public came to believe that railroad travel was safe travel. The safety record confirmed the public's belief that disasterous mishaps were not to be expected on rail travel. This naive, yet not unfounded, belief in the safety of railroading was not altogether wholesome as it turned out, for it gave the railroad companies a false sense of security. Lulled into complacency by public praise, American railroads continued to use the flimsy standards of the early period when they were immune from disasters. When the period of immunity came to a close after 1852, the companies were unwilling to make improvements in their operations or equipment. They continued to use light, flimsy cars rather than adopt more substantial coaches. Some of the earliest types of passenger coaches were retained until long after the Civil War. Because of their reluctance to improve their equipment to keep pace with increased speeds, traffic, train weights, and train lengths, railroad calamities became commonplace after 1852.

AFTER THE FATAL BOILER EXPLOSION of its first locomotive in 1831, the South Carolina Railroad placed a barrier car piled high with cotton bales between the engine and the coaches to protect the passengers lest another boiler burst.

SOMEWHERE IN SNOWY NEW ENGLAND during the 1870's this brass bound eight wheeler rolled off the rails into a field.

ONE OF THE GREATEST CATAS-TROPHES in early railroad history occurred June 28, 1859, at Mishawaka, Ind., when the Springbrook bridge broke apart from heavy rains. The Michigan Southern express bound east from Chicago late at night fell through the bridge and was pitched into the mud thirty feet below. This early photograph shows the engine and tender completely buried under the wreckage of cars. Two day coaches were smashed to pieces. The arch-roofed sleeping car survived, lying amid the wreckage. Forty-one people died in this accident.

ONE OF THE CUMBERLAND AND PENNSYLVANIA'S ungainly "Camels" went through the bridge at Wills Creek around 1865. The *Detmold* was salvaged and continued in service for many years.

THE JOHN BULL OF THE CAMDEN AND AMBOY RAILROAD was probably the first engine to be equipped with a cowcatcher (1833). Despite this safety precaution, the New Jersey line suffered many serious accidents during its early years of operations.

THIS IS THE FIRST PHOTOGRAPH ever taken of a railroad wreck. Mr. L. Wright of Pawtucket, R. I., snapped it within a few minutes of the accident which occurred in 1853. Fourteen passengers were killed in this head-on collision.

Zelda Mackay Collection

Chapter Two

The Year the Disasters Began: 1853

THE FIRST QUARTER CENTURY of relative safety in American railroad operations came to a crashing stop in 1853. In that mid-century year a series of major railroad calamities occurred that killed 234 passengers. From this starting point calamities continued to occur with striking frequency throughout the century. During the second half of the century Americans were horrified as engines derailed, bridges collapsed, boilers burst, and as trains collided and primitive car stoves ignited the debris of splintered coaches. The fearful fatality figures from rail accidents mounted through the 1860's, 1870's, 1880's, and 1890's until the early years of the new century. In 1890, for example, 6,335 people were killed and 35,362 were injured on American railroads. In 1850, only forty years earlier, there is no record of any rail fatality from a major wreck.

It seems odd that the rail disasters should begin so abruptly in 1853. Until that year no more than half a dozen passengers had been killed in any one accident. Altogether there probably had not been more than fifty passenger fatalities on American railroads. In 1853, however, a series of frightful smashups occurred. The sharp transition from the period of the railroads early years of of immunity from serious accidents to the grim period of railroad disasters is made very apparent by looking at some of the accidents that happened that fulcrum year—1853. What, though, were the causes of the deadly collisions and derailments and explosions that began that year?

One of the major causes of the change from safety to danger was cheap construction. American railroads were very cheaply built. Railroads in this country expanded rapidly after 1850, often ahead of necessary adequate capital. One solution for the problem of finance was for speculators and developers to build as cheaply as possible. American railroads as a result had many sharp curves and steep, bumpy grades, wooden rather than stone or metal bridges, and light rolling stock. Often the track was laid with little ballast under the ties, and no one seemed to pay much attention to maintenance. In the winter the track heaved high from frost, and in the spring railroad tracks were often buried in mud to the top of the rails.

The Federal Government actually encouraged flimsy railroad construction through its land grant policy, which gave railroads land and loans only as mileage was completed. As a result the government put a premium on speed in construction and length

TWO B & O PASSENGER CARS tumbled a hundred feet down a steep cliff at Cheat River, in the West Virginia mountains west of Cumberland, Md. The cars were derailed by a loose rail on April 16, 1853.

On January 6, 1853, the Boston and Maine Railroad's noon express out of Boston heading for Lawrence, Massachusetts, and carrying sixty or seventy people was derailed at Andover, Massachusetts, by a broken axle. The express had been travelling at the dizzy speed of forty miles an hour when the train fell down a steep embankment and smashed apart. The only passenger to be killed outright was the twelve-year-old son of President-elect Franklin Pierce. Gen. Pierce himself was only badly bruised, but it was reported by telegraph that he had been killed in the wreck. Newspapers all over the country headlined his death, and in Washington City Congress adjourned out of respect. The first wreck of 1853, though a minor one, was very widely publicized.

On the fourth of March 1853 a rear-end collision of the Pennsylvania Railroad in the Allegheny mountains near Mt. Union, Pennsylvania, killed seven people, the highest death toll yet in a single accident. An emigrant train had stopped because of some mechanical problem with the engine when a mail train came up from behind plunging at almost full speed into the rear car of the stationary train. The locomotive of the mail tore savagely into the emigrant car. When the steam passages of the boiler were slashed, searing steam poured in on the emigrants, scalding many in a dreadful manner. The accident seems to have been caused by gross carelessness; the brakeman, sent to the rear to signal any approaching train, sat down in a shanty and fell asleep.

And then came the disasters. Two accidents occurring only a few days apart shocked the nation. On April 25, 1853, an express and an emigrant train collided near Chicago killing twenty-one people (see Chap. 12). Then on May 6, before the public had recovered from the horror at Chicago, forty-six passengers were drowned at Norwalk, Connecticut, in the year's costliest accident when a train ran through an open drawbridge and plunged into a river. Norwalk was the first of the great bridge disasters (see Chap. 7).

The contemporary journals were severely critical about these two accidents, and public opinion, of course, ran high. An editorial in *Railroad Record* commenting on the twin disasters said: "Public feeling has been grossly outraged by these reckless sacrifices of life on railroads. Indignation meetings have been called, and several Legislatures have taken action upon the matter. We sincerely trust they

of track, not quality. In the end almost all of the government-subsidized roads were poorly built. Railroad building was very different in England. The English built their railroads with an eye for permanance and quality; their roads were designed with double track to eliminate collisions. They also built substantial stone bridges, viaducts, and tunnels, and curves and grades were eliminated. American engineers on the other hand simply laid track as rapidly as possible. Consequently, this cheap, hasty construction coupled with increased traffic and speed after 1852 produced half a century of frightful carnage.

The first rail accident in the memorable year of 1853 cannot be classed as a major disaster because only three people were killed. Still, by being the first for the year, it introduced the new era. Also one of the three fatalities was a celebrity.

PATERSON RAILROAD ACCIDENT.

A CORNFIELD MEET IN HACKENSACK MEADOW on May 9, 1853. A Paterson & Hudson River emigrant train smacked head-on into an Erie express near Secaucus, N.J., killing two people. Notice the early telegraph lines along the right-of-way.

will continue to agitate the matter until some remedy shall be applied to this great evil. Corporations have no souls, but they have pockets, and if they cannot be reached in any other way, heavy damages should be required of them in every instance where loss of life was the result of carelessness."

It seems that emigrant trains were particularly vulnerable to accidents in the nineteenth century. These overloaded westbound trains carrying newly arrived foreigners in rickety coaches frequently became involved in wrecks perhaps because they were run as specials by the railroad companies and did not meet the schedules and timetables of regularly scheduled trains. Also the companies often gave such groups the oldest, most obsolete equipment they had. Emigrant cars were normally box cars with a few windows added and hard wooden benches installed. At any rate yet another 1853 accident occurred involving an emigrant train. On May 8, two days after the grim open drawbridge at Norwalk, two trains came to-

gether in a cornfield at Secaucus, New Jersey. A Paterson and Hudson River Railroad emigrant train from Jersey City and an Erie express eastbound crashed head-on in the New Jersey countryside. Two brakemen were killed in the wreck, but fortunately no passengers died. Such head-on collisions that occurred in open country were usually called "cornfield meets."

The Secaucus smash-up was a collision between trains from two different railroads going in opposite directions on the same track. Such apparent madness can be partially explained, however. The Erie Railroad had recently acquired control of the Paterson & Hudson, and at the time of the accident the two roads were beginning to integrate their services. On the day of the collision the Paterson train left Jersey City three minutes late and stopped at the far side of Bergen Cut to wait for the Erie express, which had priority. After waiting the proper ten minutes, Conductor William Gale of the Paterson train signaled his engineer,

THE LATE ACCIDENT ON THE PENNSYLVANIA RAILROAD.

1853 WAS A BIG YEAR FOR TRAIN WRECKS. There were 138 of them in all. This rear-end collision occurred near Mt. Union, Pa., on March 4, on the Pennsylvania Road when a mail train rammed full speed into a halted emigrant train. The locomotive of the mail tore into the emigrant car, causing the steam passages to burst and scalding many in a dreadful manner.

Thomas Blakley, to proceed with caution. It was just approaching darkness in those Jersey flats, about 8:15. The light was dim, and the visibility no doubt rather obscure. Twilight concealed the two locomotives—the *Ramapo* and the *Union*—as they neared one another on that meadow. Then, before they could stop, they crashed head-on.

Out of the chaos of hissing steam and scattered mechanical debris crawled the two conductors, the bosses of their trains. Shouting in hysterical voices, they argued furiously over whose fault the wreck was. Who did have the right-of-way? Gale of the Paterson train argued that he was right. Conductor Seth Geer of the Erie express insisted that he was. Actually, neither man was in error. It was company agent H. L. Green who, in failing to notify the Paterson train of a new time schedule, was responsible for the crash. The coroner's jury placed full blame on Green; he was fired post haste.

It is sad to say that the Paterson & Hudson road continued in their careless operation after the May ninth wreck. Seven months later the same two trains, emigrant and express, crashed head-on at Secaucus within a mile of the earlier scene. The brakeman and one passenger were killed, and twenty-four passengers were seriously injured. These two collisions, both due to carelessness, show the quality of operation of many of the early roads.

Another serious collision during the year of disasters occurred on August 12, 1853, on the Providence and Worcester Railroad at Valley Falls, Rhode Island. On the morning of the twelfth an excursion train consisting of seven passenger cars was loaded with 475 holiday-goers en route to Narragansett Bay via Providence, twenty-six miles away. On the same morning a train of two passenger cars left Providence bound for Worcester. These trains, going in opposite directions, were set to pass each other on a double track siding near Pawtucket. The train out of Providence made its usual time, and on reaching Pawtucket, stopped for five minutes, according to established company regulations. It then proceeded slowly toward the single track. In rounding a sharp curve, the other train going toward

Providence came down upon it at full speed, about forty miles per hour. The two trains crashed head-on at Valley Falls Station, killing thirteen persons and seriously injuring thirty others.

The first car of the excursion was shattered; nearly every passenger was killed or badly hurt. The second car was not so badly damaged but was driven back through the third car, where casualties were also heavy. A passenger in the excursion train recorded the horror of the wreck: "I was in the sixth car of the Uxbridge train. The first intimation we had that anything was wrong was three violent jerks succeeded by a crash and, what we supposed, the explosion of the boiler. There was, of course, a general rush for the doors, and passengers ran in confusion. It seemed as though the cars had not more than come together, before a man was at work with an axe cutting into one of the windows of the second car to take out the body of a woman who had been instantly killed while attempting to escape. Two

men were hanging between the roof of the second and third cars, lifeless, and another poor fellow caught while attempting to get out of a window, was imploring for help. The wounded were taken to a grove nearby. The dead were laid upon the grass. One young man, (Goldthwait, of Uxbridge,) presented a most piteous sight. His arm was torn off near the shoulder, and he was left upon the grass, where he held up his lacerated stump, and begged for help."

The cause of the disaster was bad judgment on the part of the engineer, Edwin Gates, of the Worcester-bound train. He thought that since the excursion would be scheduled to wait five minutes at the siding he would be able to make it to the double track before the other started out. This was a fatal mistake. Even though Gates raced at full speed to make up time, he was caught on the single track with the excursion train approaching just around a sharp curve. Again the cause of heavy loss of life was human error. Referring to his accident at Valley Falls, one New York newspaper edi-

NORWALK WAS THE FIRST OF THE GREAT BRIDGE DISASTERS. On May 6, 1853, forty-six people were crushed or drowned when a New Haven Railroad train ran through an open drawbridge at Norwalk, Conn. and plunged into the Norwalk River just three hundred yards from the city depot.

THE CATASTROPHE.

THIS IS A GENERAL SCENE AT THE NORWALK DEPOT after the drawbridge catastrophe. The dead and injured were brought here for treatment and identification. Ironically, several of the fatalities were physicians returning from a medical convention.

torial concluded: "That a vast majority of railroad disasters are directly owing to the stupidity and neglect of the employees, and the apathy and avarice of the railroad officers."

An interesting sidelight of this accident is that a photograph was taken at the scene. This was the first photograph of a railroad wreck ever taken. Mr. L. Wright of Pawtucket took an excellent daguerreotype of the wreck within a few minutes of the accident. Wright's photograph was later used as a model for a woodcut

illustration of the New York *Illustrated News* of August 27, 1853.

The year 1853 was just the beginning of the railroad disasters. Year after year the railroads expanded mileage and traffic. Year after year the death toll rose. The accidents and fatalities continued for fifty years until the new century, when mechanical improvements and safety devices on trains began to lower the accident rate.

ANOTHER DRAWBRIDGE ACCIDENT in 1853 occurred on April 23 when the Camden & Amboy's two o'clock train from Philadelphia ran off the open bridge into Rancocas Creek twelve miles from the Quaker City. The draw was opened for the steamboat *Rancocas*, which is shown in the illustration; however, the bridge tender forgot to signal the engineer that the bridge was open.

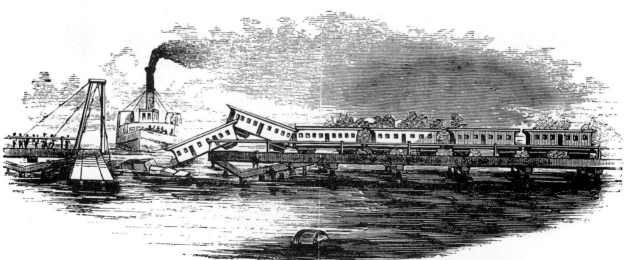

INTERIOR OF A PASSENGER-CAR AT THE MOMENT OF THE COLLISION NEAR STEAMBURG, NEW YORK.—DRAWN BY OTTO STARK.

AN ARTIST CAPTURED THE HORROR inside a passenger car at the moment of collision. The *Flying Express* of the Pennsylvania & Ohio Road has just crashed into a halted freight at the village of Steamburg, N.Y. Several passengers died in this wreck in 1888.

APPALLING DISASTER ON THE NORTHERN PENNSYLVANIA RAILROAD.

COLLISION OF THE PASSENGER AND EXCURSION TRAINS AT CAMP HILL STATION, FOURTEEN MILES FROM PHILADELPHIA. DRAWN ON THE SPOT BY OUR OWN ARTIST.

DREADFUL COLLISION OF RAILWAY TRAINS AT
CAMP HILL STATION, FOURTEEN MILES FROM PHILADELPHIA.

At five o'clock in the morning of July 17, an excursion train of ten cars left the Master street depot, Philadelphia, with the schools of St. Michael's Roman Catholic church, in Kensington. The excursion party consisted of between five and six hundred persons, the great majority of whom were children. They intended proceeding to Fort Washington, fourteen and a half miles from the city, where they were to enjoy a pic-nic. Owing to the number of cars, and the weight of the train, there was some delay, and the conductor, Mr. Alfred F. Hoppel, finding himself behind time, pushed forward with great rapidity when towards the end of his trip. The regular passenger train for the city left Gwynedd at six o'clock, and reached Camp Hill at six o'clock and eighteen minutes. Finding the excursion train had not yet arrived, Mr. Wm. Vanstavoren, the conductor, determined not to wait for it, and his train was moving along when the expected train came thundering on around a curve, at the rate of thirty-five miles an hour. A collision of course ensued with the most appalling conse-quences. The down train escaped without serious damage, but the scene presented by the excursion train was fearful. The three forward cars of the train were crushed completely to pieces, and the wreck, mingling with that of the locomotive, took fire, and the flames communicated to the other cars of the train. The two next cars after the three that were wrecked outright, took fire, and were entirely consumed. The inmates of the three forward cars were completely mixed up with the wreck, and a large number of them were killed. There were probably fifty persons in each of the three cars, and the lowest estimate fixes the number of killed a

THE FIRST OF THE GREAT RAIL HORRORS occurred at Camp Hill, Pa., when a violent head-on crash killed sixty-six young people from St. Michael's church in Philadelphia, who were on an excursion into the country. This disaster oc-curred July 17, 1856.

Collection of the Library of Congress

24

Chapter Three

The Horrors of Travel

THROUGHOUT THE NINETEENTH CENTURY America was horrified by a series of railroad catastrophes as boilers burst, bridges crumbled, and engines derailed. Wreck reports appeared frequently after 1853 in the national journals—*Harper's Weekly, Leslie's,* and *Ballou's*—publicizing the frightful cost in life and property. Every volume of these weekly magazines illustrated blood chilling artist's sketches of demolished passenger cars, twisted locomotives, and human debris. Daily newspapers also gave wide coverage by spreading gore across their front pages. It is no wonder that railroad accidents captured the imagination of the American public.

One of the earliest statements to point out the horrors of rail travel appeared in 1865 in the very respectable *Harper's Weekly*: "During the present year Death appears to have set his mark on the traveler. Everyday the record of mortality is continued. Now it is a collision; now the explosion of a locomotive, and then again the sudden precipitation of an entire train down a steep embankment or perhaps into some river. There has come to be a general insecurity and distrust, and every man or woman who steps out of a railway car unhurt does so with a feeling of sensible relief. It is a fact that more lives have been lost by accident this year than in some of the severest battles of the war [Civil]."

The names of the major rail disasters were to become household words: Camp Hill, Angola, Revere, Ashtabula, Chatsworth, Busey Bridge, Mud Run. Books were published in the bloody details of the Angola Horror and the Ashtabula Bridge Disaster; both were laced strongly with typical Victorian emotion and romanticism. A popular song recorded the holocaust at Chatsworth.

Apart from the publicity given to railroad wrecks, the possibility of disaster when one traveled by rail during the nineteenth century was a very genuine ponderable. Some experienced travellers actually made it a point to get seats in cars in the middle of a train because they believed that this mid-way location was the least vulnerable in either a head-on or rear-end collision.

The *Railroad Gazette* made an attempt to tally all railroad accidents in the United States beginning in 1873. No doubt they were able to glean the more serious accidents from the daily papers, but there was a very large number of accidents to freight trains

25

THE ANGOLA RAILROAD DISASTER—THE REAR CAR JUMPING FROM THE TRACK.—[Sketched by J. P. Hoffman.]

·   ·is agonizing cry. His mother was alive, but no one could have recognized a semblance to the human countenance in her bruised and mangled features. But the boy knew his mother, and knelt by her side, kissing her black and bleeding lips, entreating her most piteously to

"get well quick." A man, stupefied from the shock, continually asked for his wife—"Where is she? Shall I never see her again?" Fortunately she escaped with slight injuries, but in the hurry and excitement of removing the bodies the two had been carried to different houses. Her

first inquiry was after her husband, and one of the uninjured passengers, discovering the relationship, carried her news of his safety, and took back "her love" to her husband. Both recovered from their wounds.

Our third illustration on this page shows the

wreck of the second car, with the burning one in the distance under the bridge. The three in their natural order and connection fully explain and illustrate the disaster. We are indebted for one of our sketches to Mr. Erasmus W. Smith, the well-known engineer.

THE ANGOLA, N. Y., DISASTER of 1867 shocked the entire nation in its enormity. An eastbound Lake Shore express was derailed on a bridge and fell into a deep gorge. Forty-two passengers were either crushed to death or burned alive when the cars' coal stoves broke apart scattering red-hot coals about the car.

which were never reported in any newspaper. The *Gazette* records a total of 1,201 accidents in 1875. The national census report on transportation of 1880, however, reports 8,216 rail accidents that year. There is a good deal of disparity between the two sources. Although these statistics are rather meaningless in the abstract, they do indicate the frequency of train wrecks—from three to twenty-two accidents every day, depending on the source you use.

After the Civil War there began a slow improvement of some railroad equipment to reduce the terrific toll. At the same time, however, traffic became swollen; the burgeoning train traffic and increased speeds of the 1870's and 1880's took place without corresponding improvement either in the cars themselves or the roadbeds they ran over. It is true that some

THE ANGOLA DISASTER—WRECKS OF THE CARS.—[Sketched by Erasmus W. Smith.]

FRANK LESLIE'S ILLUSTRATED NEWSPAPER.

RAILROAD ACCIDENT ON THE PENNSYLVANIA ROAD NEAR MILL CREEK, PA.—THE BODY OF MRS. DUGGAN TAKEN FROM THE FLAMES

THE BODY OF MRS. DUGGAN taken from the flames of her train, which derailed in 1868 near Mill Creek, Pa. Over-turned stoves scattered live coals about the coaches, turning the wreckage into an inferno.

improvements were made; the telegraph replaced the old signal posts, but the telegraph was not universally adopted by railroads until late in the century. Rails, too, were gradually improved after the Civil War, but many lines failed to replace old strap- or wrought-iron rail with steel until after disastrous derailments. As safety devices were developed, the speeds at which passenger trains traveled accelerated. As Lucius Beebe said, "The grim reaper has never been altogether outdistanced by progress."

The first of the real horrors was at Camp Hill near Philadelphia on the North Pennsylvania Railroad (now the Reading). A violent head-on collision of an excursion train killed sixty-six, the most overwhelming disaster in American railroad history. Excursion trains, like emigrant trains, were especially subject to serious mishaps. The Camp Hill collision is a particularly sad example of such a disaster.

In the early hours of Thursday, July 17, 1856, the young people of Philadelphia's St. Michael's Church boarded two special excursion trains that would take them fifteen miles into the countryside for a picnic-outing at Fort Washington. Nearly 1,500 children climbed aboard the trains that morning, representing almost every family in the parish. There were of course delays in loading these exuberant Irish-American children. The first train with 600 youngsters pulled out at 5:30 a.m., half an hour late, pulled by the locomotive *Shackamaxon* with twenty-one-year-old Henry Harris at the throttle.

Meanwhile, the regular train lead by the *Aramingo* bound for Philadelphia left Fort Washington at 6:14 a.m. with Conductor William Vanstavoren in charge. Just as this regular train had entered a curve near Camp Hill, the St. Michael's Parish excursion train appeared, running at 35 miles an hour. The two trains plowed together with a thunderous roar. Although no one in the regular train was hurt, the special had become an inferno. Coals from the fireboxes of the engines mingled with the wood debris of the smashed cars, and the wreckage immediately caught fire. Five cars of the excursion burned quickly. Sixty-six young

A HORRENDOUS PILE-UP OF CARS of an Old Colony Railroad excursion train after a derailment near Boston. A misplaced switch caused the accident which killed twenty-five passengers in October of 1878.

passengers were incinerated. Camp Hill was far and away the very worst railroad accident that had occurred in America's history.

Immediately after the collision Conductor Vanstavoren, who was uninjured, jumped aboard a carriage and dashed for his home in Philadelphia, where in intense grief and guilt he took a dose of poison. Naturally, the press seized upon the Camp Hill disaster to continue their vituperation against the railroads. The *New York Times* used the banner headline "Railroad Butchery" to berate the company.

America's most notorious railroad disasters happened at Angola, New York, and Ashtabula, Ohio. Both accidents involved faulty bridges and dreadful fires. Both accidents secured a strong hold on the public imagination.

On December 18, 1867, an eastbound Lake Shore express, running fast to make up time, was derailed at Three Sisters Creek near Angola, New York. The cause of the derailment was a defective axle on the rear car. Just before the train passed over the bridge, a wheel on the bent axle struck a frog in the track. The rear car instantly jumped the track and bumped along the ties, being pulled along by the train. Then the car just ahead was derailed by the jolting and pulling of the last car. A moment before reaching the bridge the last car became uncoupled and fell against the bridge abutment. The car's coal stove broke apart in the concussion scattering red-hot coals about the car and passengers. The fire spread rapidly in the old wooden coach. Forty-two passengers were burned alive. The other derailed car was dragged along the track some 300 feet; then it too broke loose and fell down an embankment. Though the second car was badly smashed, only one passenger was killed.

Scenes of the charred bodies of the Angola

THE ASHTABULA DISASTER was the most deadly railroad accident in the United States up to that time. On Dec. 29, 1876, the Lake Shore's crack *Pacific Express* plunged through the high bridge at Ashtabula, Ohio, carrying eighty passengers to fiery deaths. The disaster so shocked the nation that this memorial lithograph was published. It shows the locomotive *Columbia*, the enginemen, and scenes of the fatal bridge before and after the disaster.

victims were ghoulishly spread across newspapers and magazines across the country. A mass funeral was held for the dead in the Exchange Street Depot in Buffalo just three days before Christmas 1867. It is no wonder that this accident became popularly known as "The Angola Horror."

The Ashtabula Bridge Disaster, another Christmastime wreck, took place on the same road as the Angola Horror—Commodore Vanderbilt's Lake Shore Road, which ran from Buffalo to Chicago. On the snowy winter night of December 29, 1876, the Lake Shore's Pacific Express plunged through a high bridge at Ashtabula, Ohio, carrying eighty passengers to a fiery doom. This was the most deadly accident up to that time.

On the night of the accident the train proceeded across Ashtabula Bridge with caution because of the low visibility from the snow storm. Just as the front wheels of the engine *Socrates* touched the firm ground of the far bank, the engineer heard a cracking sound and

felt the bridge begin to tremble. Immediately he opened his throttle full, and his engine jumped ahead and off the bridge. Looking behind, the engineer saw that his engine was separated from the rest of the train. All the cars to the rear had plunged into the deep ravine. Car fell on top of car in a great heap. Red-hot car stoves ignited the splintered wreckage turning the pile of cars into a colossal bonfire. Of nearly 200 passengers 80 perished. Nineteen victims were so badly burned that they were never identified.

This holiday disaster shocked the country. The Ohio Legislature began its own investigation to determine why the bridge should fall down under an ordinary load. Engineers who examined the plans and remains of the bridge explained that the bridge was indeed faulty. In fact, they were surprised that it had held up as long as it had—eleven years. Amasa Stone, president of the Cleveland & Erie Railroad, had designed the bridge and was clearly responsible. Stone was a partner with his brother-in-

29

ARTIST SKETCHES OF THE INFAMOUS MUD RUN DISASTER of 1888 illustrate the contemporary taste for sensational journalism. View 1 shows the wreck shortly after the rear-end collision. Rescuers are still at work dragging out bodies. The dead lie in rows beside the track. View 3 shows the bodies of the victims stacked together in the funeral car. The gore was exquisite. In View 2 the injured are being removed to the Mud Run hotel.

law, Elias Howe, in the Howe Bridge and Truss Company. As Stone was a prominent business executive, he was not prosecuted. Public opinion, however, was against him, and he committed suicide a few years after the Ashtabula tragedy.

Another accident to illustrate the horrors of rail travel during the last half of the nineteenth century was the Chatsworth wreck, which happened on the Toledo, Peoria & Western Railroad near Chatsworth, Illinois, on August 10, 1887. The victims were on an excursion train bound from the farmlands of central Illi-

nois for Niagara Falls. Eighty-two of the group were killed, more than at Ashtabula. A bridge was the cause of the wreck, not a great structure as at Ashtabula, but just an insignificantly small fifteen foot wooden trestle over a shallow culvert that was dry most of the year.

Since the excursion had left Peoria late, at about midnight, Engineer Sutherland was running faster than usual. A bit past Chatsworth Sutherland saw what appeared to be a brush fire ahead near the track. Then he realized that it was the trestle itself that was afire. Quickly he reversed his engine and whistled for brakes too late. He couldn't stop or even slow down very much. On the train rolled across the blazing trestle at thirty-five miles an hour. The lead engine made it across safely, but under the weight of the second locomotive the wooden span collapsed, toppling into the creek. Then the following nine cars fell upon it in a smashed, mangled pile. The tenth car, a sleeper, stopped with one end just over the burning trestle. The second sleeper completely telescoped the first, killing almost all of the passengers in both cars.

Like most wrecks this one could have been prevented. The day before the tragedy Timothy Coughlan and his railroad gang had been burning weeds along the track. At quitting time Coughlan cautioned his men to be sure the fire was out. As it was a dry summer in Illinois, some of the fire must have remained smoldering. Coughlan did not patrol his track to check to see that the fire was out before the excursion train came along. His neglect led to the fire and the loss of eighty-two lives.

The wreck at Chatsworth so much impressed the people in the Middle West that they made it a part of their regional folklore. T. P. Westendorf wrote a song about it called "The Bridge Was Burned at Chatsworth." One of the particularly vivid stanzas goes:

> *The mighty crash of timbers*
> *A sound of hissing steam*
> *The groans and cries of anguish*
> *A woman's stifled scream.*
> *The dead and dying mingled,*
> *With broken beams and bars*
> *An awful human carnage*
> *A dreadful wreck of cars.*

The public outcry against lax safety standards on the railroads led the Federal Government to begin an official investigation of accidents. In 1901 the roads were required to report all collisions and derailments to the Interstate Commerce Commission (ICC). In 1910 railroad companies were further required to report to ICC all accidents involving injury or property damage; ICC was at that time also given power to make their own investigation of a serious railroad accident. Today this government investigation is handled by the U.S. Dept. of Transportation.

THE BUSEY BRIDGE collapsed suddenly one morning in 1887, killing twenty-four commuters and school children on their way into Boston. The bridge was proved to be totally unsafe.

THE CHATSWORTH, ILL. WRECK of Aug. 10, 1887, illustrates the many horrors of rail travel during the last half of the nineteenth century. Eighty-two passengers on a gala Toledo & Peoria excursion train were killed when a small fire-weakened bridge over a culvert collapsed under the weight of the engine. Nine wooden coaches were crushed into a horrible mass.

Collection of the Library of Congress

THIS IS THE SMALL BRIDGE that collapsed at Chatsworth resulting in eighty-two deaths.

HARPER'S WEEKLY.

JOURNAL OF CIVILIZATION.

VOL. XXXI.—No. 1600.
Copyright, 1887, by HARPER & BROTHERS.

NEW YORK, SATURDAY, AUGUST 20, 1887.

TEN CENTS A COPY.
$4.00 PER YEAR, IN ADVANCE

"THE AIR RESOUNDED with the shrieks, groans and prayers of the sufferers," as rescuers worked feverishly to save the wounded and dying from amid the shattered wreckage of the terrible disaster at Chatsworth.

AFTER ENGINE 13 FELL THROUGH THE BURNING BRIDGE, it rolled into a culvert. The following cars fell on top of it, breaking apart in a shocking manner. The roof of one car lies totally separated from the body.

THE NEW YORK CENTRAL'S LAKE SHORE LTD. sped around a curve at Little Falls, N.Y., jumped the track, and plowed into a rock wall. Thirty persons were killed in this crash on April 19, 1940.

Derailments

T RAINS WERE FOREVER running off the track on the pioneer railroads. Some tickets even imprinted an agreement making the passenger subject to call if needed to replace the engine or cars on the rails. But since rail travel was a novelty during the 1830's and 1840's and because the rolling stock was very light, the passengers took occasional derailments in their stride. This contemporary account shows what railroad rides could be like in 1840.

On Tuesday, February 4, J. S. Buckingham, visiting America from England, left Philadelphia for Harrisburg at 7 am. By 2 pm he had arrived in Lancaster. "From Lancaster to Harrisburg it [the railroad] has been so badly constructed that accidents are continually happening by the cars getting off the track, by upsetting and by other modes by which passengers are often injured and sometimes killed," he wrote. On his return trip to Philadelphia he describes the effects of that 1840 winter on the track.

"The frost having broken up and all the heavy snow on the ground melted, the road was in the most miry condition possible and in some places the rails were nearly covered with mud. So much extra caution was necessary in this state of things that we could not proceed at a greater rate than eight miles an hour and even then we were thrown off the track several times and on each occasion getting the engine and cars on again was a work of considerable delay and difficulty. It was quite dark when we reached Philadelphia and we thought it the most disagreeable journey by railroad we have ever performed, though we were told that we ought to congratulate ourselves on not having been upset when thrown off the track or detained for eight or ten hours before we could get in again."

One of the chief causes of derailments in the past and right up to the present time is broken or faulty rail. Although the first railroads in America tried their best to build firm, sturdy tracks to run their trains over, many of the roads were primitive and insecure. As the stumpy trains trundled along, a dip, bend, or twist in the road was often enough to derail the cars. Usually, since speeds were low, little damage was done; the cars were simply replaced on the tracks and the train went along its way. However, if the derailment happened near a bridge or an embankment, the harmless derailment could be turned into a major disaster.

Most of the first tracks in America were laid with "strap" rail, which was constructed by placing long iron straps on top of wooden beams. Since timber was cheap and plentiful in this country and iron was scarce and expensive, the "strap" rail was an expedient. Also "strap" rail was the only form of rail that could be rolled in American mills up to 1844; consequently, "strap" rail was used from 1830 to 1850. A defect of the "strap" rail was that the rolling action of the train wheels tended to bend the iron straps so that eventually they worked loose. Then the spikes would not hold, and the end of the rail with its sharp point could stick up far enough to become caught under a wheel, rip it up from the wooden sill, and tear through the floor of a car. These "snakeheads," as they were called, created havoc when they tore into a car full of passengers.

There is an early account of a "snakehead" which slashed into a passenger car on the Portsmouth and Roanoke Railroad in Virginia and caused the train to derail. On the tenth of December, 1837, a train of cars was headed for Halifax, Virginia, with eight passenger cars and several loads of produce. The contemporary account of the "snakehead" accident goes like this: "In their progress they encountered the end of one of the iron rails, the spike or

bolt of which had started, or the end rusted off, so that the end projected above the level of the road. It is stated that the inequality was so slight that the wheels would have easily passed over it, but it was caught by a strong iron fender, which travelled before the wheel, and bent up; and consequently the engine was thrown off the track. The headway of the passenger-cars being thus stopped, they were run into by the burden-cars, and ten persons injured, two of whom have since died."

A remedy to the dangerous strap rail was sought as early as 1840. Robert L. Stevens, president and chief engineer of the Camden & Amboy Railroad, presented a solution to the problem by designing the "tee" rail, which was solid iron and a great improvement over strap rail. After Stevens first installed his English-made rail on his own line in 1831, "tee" rail became popular on most first-class roads. On branch lines or cheaply constructed ones, however, strap rails were used until well after the Civil War.

In spite of the definite improvements of solid metal rail, wrought iron was not really heavy enough to stand up under the abuse of heavy trains and the severe winters in America. Iron rails were brittle and wore out fast. The answer was, of course, steel. By 1862 Hen-

ALL IN PIECES this elegant 4-4-0 lies belly-up with her sunflower stack in the foreground.

ry Bessemer's process of steel making was just coming into use in Great Britain. The first steel rail in this country was laid in 1863 by the Pennsylvania Railroad, which imported 150 tons from England. In 1865 a Chicago steel mill was the first to roll Bessemer steel rails here. At that time the more prosperous and more heavily travelled roads began to substitute steel for iron rails. By the end of the 1880's the long-wearing steel had pretty well replaced iron, making it possible for the railroads to run much longer and heavier trains more safely than ever before.

The rapid improvement in rails did not eliminate the threat of derailments; they remained prolific during the nineteenth century and continue up to the present. Obviously, not all derailments are caused by faulty track. High speeds on a curve, an obstruction on the track, a misplaced switch, broken running gear, a wash-out, or boiler explosion—all these could bring about a derailment.

A defective rail caused a serious derailment on the Erie Railroad on April 15, 1868. In going around a sharp curve at Carr's Point, New York, the train ran onto a broken rail.

Four passenger cars were thrown from the track and rolled down a 100 foot embankment into a ravine. The first car was crushed in the fall, and the others rolled down on top of it. Overturned stoves then set fire to the wreckage. Twenty-six persons were killed and sixty-three injured. A *Harper's Weekly* editorial severely condemned the Erie management, "as guilty of the frightful massacre. We mean exactly what we say. The train was running at an extraordinary speed on what is naturally the most dangerous part of the road."

The possibility of derailment at a bridge is especially dire. One example of such an accident was the grim holocaust on the Vermont

MUCH OF THE FIRST RAILROAD TRACK in this country was laid on "strap" rail, which was made by placing heavy iron straps on top of wooden beams. Though cheap and easy to construct, this "strap" rail often worked loose from its sills and caused derailments. This illustration shows a section of B & O "strap" rail dating from 1829.

RAILROAD ACCIDENT IN KENTUCKY.

PASSENGERS, MOSTLY UNION SOLDIERS, jump to safety as a "snakehead" rips into the floor of their car on the Louisville & Nashville Road near Lebanon Jct., Ky. These "snakeheads" were not uncommon in the days when most lines were built with "strap" rail.

Central in 1887. On the morning of February 5, a six-car train was carrying about eighty passengers, many on their way to visit the winter carnival at Montreal. As the train rolled across the 650-foot-long bridge spanning the White River, near the village of West Hartford, Vermont, the rear coach *Pilgrim* and the three preceding cars catapulted off the bridge into the stream sixty feet below. Immediately the splintered cars caught fire. Although the engine crew and the passengers from the two unharmed cars hurried down the bank, they were not able to rescue more than a few victims. Thirty-two died, many from the fire; others drowned in the frigid stream. The cause of the tragedy was a broken rail about 200 feet before the bridge. No doubt the extremely cold weather weakened the metal enough to cause it to snap under the weight of the train.

Another New England rail disaster on August 19, 1890, was caused by a heavy jack left

A SYSTEM OF INTERLOCKING SWITCHES which came into widespread use by the 1890's did much to reduce the hazard of derailment caused by misplaced switches. With this improved method a single switchman could control dozens of switches from his tower.

Interior of a Switch-tower, showing the Operation of Interlocking Switches.

ROUNDING A CURVE TOO FAST in the Chicago Yards, this Pennsylvania locomotive and tender jumped the tracks on Sept. 16, 1941. Notice how the trucks of the tender remained on the track.

ANOTHER VIEW of the Chicago Yards derailment.

ON DEC. 26, 1885, a New York, New Haven and Hartford engine, tender, and mail were derailed near the Pelhamville station by faulty track.

on the track by a gang of laborers who had been at work reballasting the roadbed near Quincy, Mass. A speeding Boston-bound Vineyard, Nantucket & Hyannis Express struck the jack at about forty miles an hour. The engine was immediately derailed but continued ahead 280 feet further, then fell over on its side. The momentum drove the following cars ahead, crashing into the engine. One car was crushed onto the engine, which then burst its steam pipes and sprayed searing steam into the heavily loaded coach. Twenty-three passengers were killed. The accident seems especially tragic because it was caused entirely by human negligence.

A more recent serious derailment in New York State was caused by high speed on a sharp curve. Fifteen minutes late on its New York-Chicago run, the crack Lake Shore Limited of the New York Central Railroad raced

THE DENVER AND RIO GRAND'S Baldwin ten-wheeler lost her smoke box, front end, and headlight in climbing off the rails onto a pile of ties.

LYING SEDATELY IN A FIELD near San Marcos, Texas, these Missouri, Kansas & Texas Railroad Pullmans piled up after derailing from a broken rail on Sept. 16, 1914.

up the Mohawk Valley about noon on April 19, 1940. There was a driving rain coming down. Near Little Falls, New York, engineers are required to slow down to forty-five miles per hour for Gulf Curve, sharpest on the entire New York Central System. However, the engineer failed to reduce his speed. Going into the curve the express was hitting fifty-nine. The locomotive jumped the track, hurtled over two other tracks, crashed head-on into a rock wall, and exploded. Nine cars piled up like straws behind it.

In the first two Pullmans rescuers found mostly mangled bodies. In the next two were the worst injured. By noon next day there were thirty known dead, including the engineer, Jesse Earl, and a hundred wounded. The last car, though derailed, was unharmed. It was occupied by thirty-five Chinese being deported from the country. This accident at Little Falls is a sad contrast with the safety record of United States airlines, which finished the year 1940 without a single fatality.

FREEZING WINDS HAMPERED THE MEN of this big Oregon Railroad & Navigation Company wrecking hook as it pulled the derailed cars out of an icy stream near Meacham Creek, Ore. in February of 1903.

Collection of the Library of Congress

THE ROCKY CANYON WALLS and roaring mountain stream witnessed this derailment at Golden, Colo. on the Union Pacific, Denver, and Gulf Railroad. An overloaded baggage car rolled over the tiny narrow gauge track dragging the engine with it in August, 1895.

THE WRECKING CREW shored up the Louisville & Nashville's 256 before the photographer snapped her portrait amid the ruined freight cars.

A SHORT FREIGHT derailed on the Fitchburg Railroad some time in the 1890's near Millers Falls, Mass. The Mogul freight engine headed down the bank for the stream, but a few of the cars preferred the up-hill journey to the woods.

BUCKING THE SNOW on the Boston & Maine at Farmington, N.H. in the winter of 1906.

THE GRAND TRUNK'S 423 went off the rails at Island Point, Vt. in 1894. Note the bent main rod.

ON HER SIDE ACROSS THE MAIN LINE, this light Pacific undoubtedly blocked the tracks for days. One of the heavy Pullmans following her came to rest on top of the upset tender.

AFTER STRIKING A BOULDER on the track near Pittsburgh, this PRR Pacific and its tender plunged over a retaining wall onto the street fifty-six feet below. Fortunately, the coaches, though derailed, remained on the track. The derailment happened on Christmas Day, 1937.

DERAILED BY A CARELESS TRACK BOSS who was satisfied that a temporary switch repair was "good enough" put Number 42 of the Central New England Railroad on her side in September 1907 near Lloyd, N. Y.

A SANTA FE WESTBOUND PASSENGER TRAIN with two locomotives and fourteen cars tore around a curve at Domingo, N. Mex. on July 3, 1923, and careened off the track. Killed in the wreck were both the engineers and both firemen; forty-five passengers were badly injured.

A HEAVY LIMA-BUILT MIKADO rolled off the Nickle Plate bridge approach at Layfayette, Ind., in February 1948.

THE LOCAL RESIDENTS were fascinated to see this helpless beast lying on her back after derailing at Ashokan, N. Y.

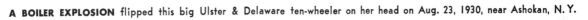

A BOILER EXPLOSION flipped this big Ulster & Delaware ten-wheeler on her head on Aug. 23, 1930, near Ashokan, N. Y.

NO PROOF OF SABOTAGE but this pile-up of tank cars near Cresson, Pa. caused many questions in the war-weary America of 1942.

THE DELAWARE AND HUDSON'S 1617, a huge Mallet freight engine, derailed in June 1945. Workmen watch as she is uprighted.

FIVE PASSENGERS WERE SUFFOCATED by salt brine when this Long Island Railroad train was derailed and cracked into a storage tank containing thousands of gallons of brine preservative. A defective switch caused this accident at Calverton, N. Y., on Aug. 13, 1926.

STEAM WHEEZING AT EVERY JOINT, the brawny, big hook strains in unison with the crew to clear the tracks. A good many steam rigs are still in service today.

THIS BRAND NEW MISSOURI AND PACIFIC locomotive dropped off the rails and chewed up the cinders for about fifteen feet after falling on her side. Notice how the 225-ton engine twisted the rails in her fall. The derailment occurred at Hoisington, Kan.

THE BLUNT NOSE of this General Motors "A" unit was flattened at the Dorsey, Ark., accident on the K.C.S.

OUR VICTORIAN GRANDPARENTS loved bird's-eye views, but this modern panorama shows no idealized scene. A long line of steel cars derailed at Warsaw, Indiana, in April 1947.

SUPPER WAS JUST BEGINNING when the Kansas City Southern's No. 50 freight derailed in a shattering thunder of mangled steel at Dorsey, Arkansas in the early winter of 1948.

EXCESSIVE SPEED WAS THE CAUSE of the costly Woodbridge, N. J. derailment of Feb. 6, 1951. Eighty-four persons were killed in the accident. In spite of their steel construction four coaches of this Pennsey commuter were severely damaged.

THIS MESSY DERAILMENT, at the height of wartime traffic, stopped all trains from entering the Baltimore tunnel. The scene is near Camden Station, Baltimore, December 1943.

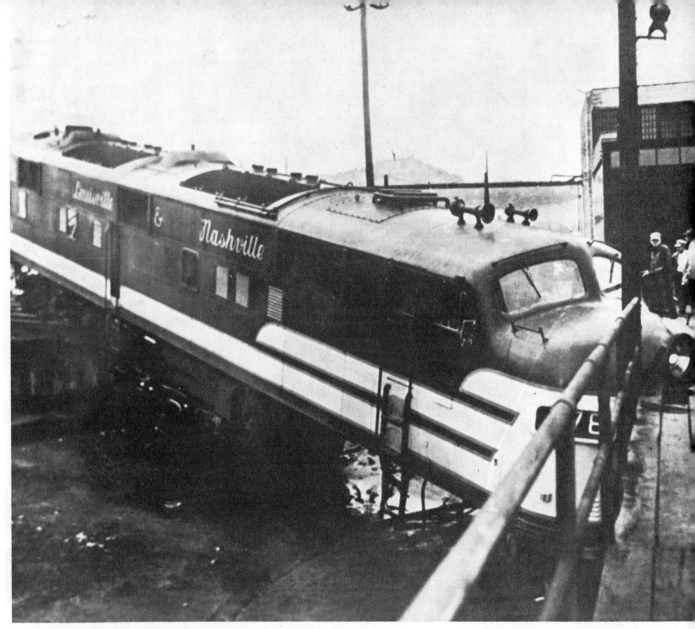

THIS LOUISVILLE & NASHVILLE diesel-electric passenger locomotive plunged into a turntable pit in the Cincinnati Yards in 1957, spilling 12,000 gallons of fuel oil.

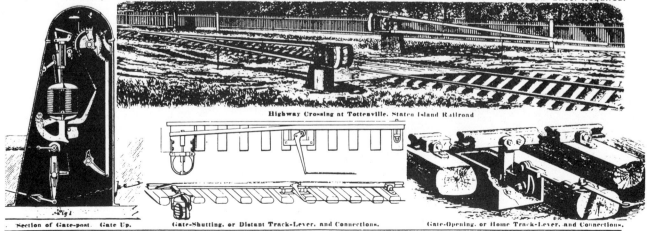

A GOOD CLOSE UP of a "cornfield meet" on the Boston & Maine shows how one engine actually penetrated the other in the collision. The cab of the engine at the right was splintered by the impact.

Chapter Five

Head-On Collisions

Head-on collisions were common in the early days of railroading in America. At the time when almost all railroads consisted of single track, it was inevitable that they should occasionally meet. The company's only method of controlling rail traffic on these single lines where trains travelled in both directions was the timetable. To avoid collisions, each railroad devised its own timetable to establish exactly where each of its trains was to be on the line at a particular time.

Timetable scheduling of trains was primitive, but remember, there was no other way to control train movement. Until the 1850's when the telegraph came into use, there was no way to communicate from one train to another or from one station to another. Once a train had departed from one station, it was on its own until it arrived at another station, where it could get further orders.

The timetables were meant to be as exact as possible, and they were to be rigidly followed by the train crew. The timetable, for instance, established points where trains travelling in opposite directions could meet at appointed times and pass each other or where a fast express could overtake a slow freight at a "turnout." Ideally, the timetable controlled the many trains on a single track and kept traffic running smoothly. In reality, however, the success of the timetable in rail operations was dependent entirely on the men who ran the trains. It was liable to many handicaps: fog might cause delays; there were frequent breakdowns; engineers or conductors failed to follow orders.

One such instance when a conductor failed to follow a prescribed timetable resulted in a head-on smashup on the Long Island Railroad at the end of the Civil War. On August 28, 1865, *General Grant* and *General Sherman* collided in a pasture at Jamaica, New York. Five passengers were killed in this cornfield meet. On the morning of the twenty-eighth the mail train going east left Winfield for Jamaica thirty five minutes late, at 9:20 am. An express going west started from Jamaica to Winfield at 9:35 am. This latter train had been out two minutes when it smashed head-on into the mail. The conductor of the mail failed to observe timetable orders. Knowing that he was late, he should have sent a flagman ahead to warn the approaching train as the rules of the company prescribed.

The timetable era of railroad traffic control lasted twenty-five years, until 1855. By

A HEAD-ON COLLISION in New England wrecked three fine old engines and killed four crewmen in 1889.

the Civil War some of the largest companies began to dispatch trains by telegraph. However, many railroads were not as swift in adopting the telegraph as one would think. Even by 1880 head-on accidents continued to occur from timetable errors because some roads were reluctant to install expensive telegraph wires. In his book *Notes on Railroad Accidents* Charles Francis Adams scolded railroad owners for their stupid conservatism in failing to adopt the telegraph.

Another problem to confuse train movements and to make operations dangerous was the lack of standard time in America. Before 1883 trains were run in a crazy pattern of dozens of times based on several local sun times. For example, when it was noon in Chicago, it was 11:27 a.m. in Omaha; 11:50 in St. Louis; 12:09 p.m. in Louisville; 12:17 in Toledo, and 12:31 in Pittsburgh. In Pittsburgh there were six different times for departures and arrivals

of trains. The train station in Buffalo had three clocks, each with a different railroad time. There were twenty-seven local times in Illinois; thirty-eight in Wisconsin. It is no wonder that serious accidents resulted from a train's failure to follow timetable orders with the absence of any unity of time.

The timetable system was a factor in a number of early head-on collisions already discussed in previous chapters: Secaucus, New Jersey, 1853; Valley Falls, Rhode Island, 1853; Camp Hill, Pennsylvania, 1856. After the Civil War, as mileage multiplied and traffic burgeoned, head-on collisions grew quite frequent. The length of trains was also much longer than before, and, of course, with such increased weight trains were difficult to stop as they were dependent on primitive hand brakes. The *Railroad Gazette* reported 104 head-on collisions in 1875.

Just Time to Jump.

DURING A VIOLENT SNOWSTORM in the winter of 1887 a freight engine climbed up on the boiler of a snow plow as if it were a steep grade, leaving the front truck and pilot buried in the plow. The smoke box, stack, and upper works of the engine pushing the plow were demolished.

THE RESULT OF A COLLISI▨
between a Snow-plough a▨
Milk Train, February 4,▨
at Marlboro Junction, M▨

AFTER THE BLIZZARD SUBSIDED, the people of Marlboro Jct., Mass. looked out of their windows to find a milk train perched on top of a locomotive that was pushing a snow plow on the Clinton & Fitchburg Branch of the New Haven Railroad. The engines struck each other so hard that the plow scooped up the milk train's engine and carried it onto her shoulders. The freak accident happened on Feb. 4, 1898.

On the morning of September 14, 1886, an eastbound Nickle Plate excursion train was carrying members of the Methodist Church of Erie, Pennsylvania, to a holiday at Niagara Falls. Train orders called for the excursion to pass a westbound freight at Silver Creek, New York. The engineer of the excursion, however, went through Silver Creek without stopping. As a result the two trains rammed head-on in a sharp curve. Although neither engine was badly damaged, telescoping of the cars caused great loss of life. The baggage car of the excursion train completely telescoped the smoking car, where twenty passengers, all men, were killed. In 1886 ladies did not ride in smoking cars.

The Silver Creek collision was clearly the result of disobeying orders. The engineer and conductor of the excursion were indicted for manslaughter for countermanding dispatcher's orders. Perhaps if the company had used the telegraph to notify trains of movements, the calamity would have been avoided.

The danger of a head-on collision is not eliminated on railroads with double track. Such accidents can occur as well on multiple track if a train is derailed and fouls the path of another. Such incidents of blocking the path of another train are especially dangerous on heavily trafficked lines where trains run at frequent intervals, often at speeds of 70 or 80 miles per hour.

58

On the night of March 27, 1953, such a collision occurred on the busy multiple track on the New York Central Railroad near Conneaut, Ohio. Four trains were involved on the four track line. As two freight trains were passing each other in opposite directions, a flagman on the caboose of the westbound train 1736 noticed sparks flying from the running gear of a car on the eastbound freight 1871. As he signaled this news, a passenger train, *The Mohawk,* bound west, began to overtake and pass No. 1736. This passenger train traveling at 76 miles an hour very suddenly swerved and plunged into the side of the freight. The passenger train was totally derailed as was most of freight 1736. Wrecked cars and debris were scattered over the multiple track.

Just a moment after this side collision the *Southwestern Ltd.,* coming at seventy miles an hour, smashed into the wreckage. Eight cars of the two passenger trains were demolished: the first two cars from the *Southwestern* and the first six from the *Mohawk.* Nine more cars of the *Southwestern* were derailed. Twenty-one passengers were killed in the violent collision.

The cause of the multiple wreck was improperly loaded cargo. A load of metal pipe on a gondola car, not securely loaded, fell from the car. One section of the thirteen-inch pipe fell on the adjacent track. This piece of pipe is what caused the *Mohawk* to swerve into the freight.

One interesting sidelight to the discussion of head-on train wrecks is the staged "cornfield meets" that were held at fairs and expositions in the 1890's and early years of the twentieth century. Crowds paid a dollar or more for the thrill of seeing two iron behemoths run together at full speed. One of the earliest staged wrecks drew 89,000 spectators at the 1896 Iowa State Fair at Des Moines. Evidently there is something in most people that attracts them to

ANOTHER FREAKISH HEAD-ON COLLISION of Feb. 18, 1885, produced this bizzare posturing of two locomotives on the New York Central and Hudson Railroad near Batavia, N.Y.   *Collection of the Library of Congress*

all sorts of disasters—fires, wrecks, and riots. There must have been some sort of carthesis as the crowd gathered to watch the terrific smash-up of these locomotives from the safe distance of a grand stand—a bit like witnessing *Macbeth* from the first gallery.

One man made a business of staging head-on collisions of steam engines, mostly 4-4-0's, all over the country. For thirty-six years "Head-On Joe" Connolly scheduled "cornfield meets" for a paid admission. Altogether he wrecked 146 locomotives in seventy-three spectacles. Sometimes he attached an old wooden coach to each engine. The coaches were saturated with gasoline, and each one contained a pot of burning charcoal. The impact upset the pots, and the coaches burst into flames. The crowds loved it.

THERE'S NOT MUCH LEFT of these locomotives of the Maine Central. After running into each other at Riverside, Me., in 1883, both boilers burst, killing the crews and blowing the engines to pieces.

FRANK LESLIE'S ILLUSTRATED NEWSPAPER.

JUNE 20, 1874.]

DANGER SIGNAL ON THE ERIE RAILWAY.—THE TORPEDO.—"DOWN BRAKES!"—SEE PAGE 238.

THE INVENTION OF THE TORPEDO SIGNAL about 1874 was helpful in preventing collisions. Torpedos are small discs filled with detonating powder and fitted with tin straps that can be bent down to clasp over the top of the rail. The torpedo is a useful signal even in dense fog because it explodes with a loud report when struck by a locomotive wheel, thus clearly signaling the engineer of danger ahead.

A MISPLACED SWITCH on the New York City Elevated Railroad caused these trains to ram together on March 25, 1879, at the 42nd Street Station. *Collection of the Library of Congress*

NEW YORK CITY.—COLLISION OF TRAINS ON THE EAST SIDE LINE OF THE NEW YORK ELEVATED RAILROAD, AT FORTY-SECOND STREET, MARCH 25TH.

STAGED WRECKS DREW THOUSANDS OF SPECTATORS at fairs and expositions around the turn of the century. The crowds were thrilled by the sight as two iron monsters charged toward each other destined for disaster.

Collection of the Library of Congress

CRUNCHED DIESEL UNITS after a head-on collision of two Southern Railroad freights which met on a curve near Eufola, N.C., on June 21, 1963. Misreading of train orders caused the smash.

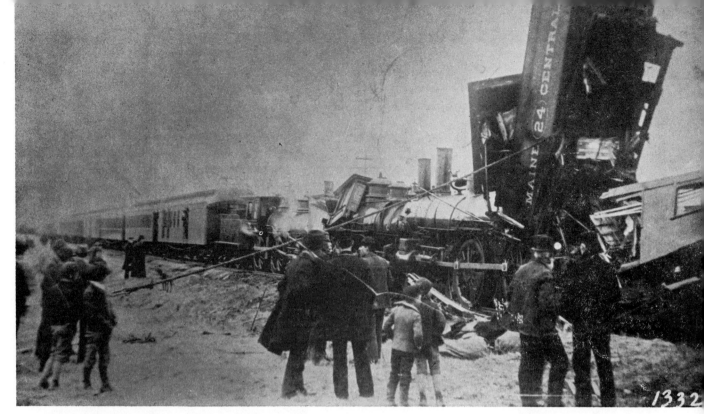

A DISPATCHER'S ERROR caused this disastrous head-on wreck on the Maine Central at Veazie, Me., in 1895. Three engines and two baggage cars were demolished.

EMBRACED AS IN DEADLY STRIFE, the *Lyons* and the *Lucifer* of the Chicago and Northwestern Railway battle it out after meeting on April 29, 1874, near the town of Franklin Grove, Ill. A signal error caused the wreck.

THIS NEW HAVEN LOCOMOTIVE lies helpless in a tidal swamp near Kingston, R. I., after colliding with the wreck of a freight train whose boiler had exploded just minutes before. Since the crew of the freight were all killed in the explosion, no one could go ahead to flag the *Cape Codder*. The accident happened on June 26, 1926.

THESE TWO BIG STEAMERS rammed together during the night of March 28, 1916 at Lemon Springs, N. C.

THE DERAILMENT AND COLLISION of the *Penn Flyer* at Ft. Wayne, Ind. on Aug. 13, 1911.

JUST AFTER THE PENNSYLVANIA'S *Penn Flyer* derailed, another freight came along and plowed into the wreckage. Four were killed and fifty-seven injured in the collision in 1911.

A HEAD-ON COLLISION at Lander, Calif. on Sept. 9, 1892, on the Southern Pacific, smashed up a solid train of early refrigerator cars carrying California fruit to the east coast.

ANOTHER VIEW of the Lander, Calif. collision of 1892.

A TRIPLE WRECK at Conneaut, Ohio, on March 27, 1953, killed 21 people when two passenger trains and a freight of the New York Central collided.

THE RUINS OF THREE TRAINS litter the New York Central roadway near Conneaut, Ohio, in 1953.

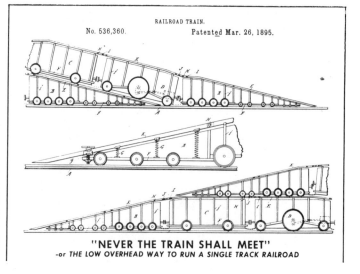

RAILROAD TRAIN.

No. 536,360.   Patented Mar. 26, 1895.

"NEVER THE TRAIN SHALL MEET"
-or *THE LOW OVERHEAD WAY TO RUN A SINGLE TRACK RAILROAD*

THROUGHOUT THE NINETEENTH CENTURY men were searching for a way to eliminate the frightful head-on collision. One ingenious scheme was proposed in 1895 by a man from Wilkes, Montana. It offered a sort of leap-frog contraption by which trains could climb over one another via an inclined plane and roof-mounted tracks. The usefulness of this device was wide and varied according to the inventor. Fast trains could pass slow freights. Head-on smashups could be entirely eliminated. A single track could serve the entire line, and a rollicking roller-coaster excitement would add thrills for the passengers.

WRECKS WERE FREQUENT ON MID-CENTURY RAILROADS. What with bridge collapses, washouts, derailments, and collisions, death was a very real ponderable for the locomotive engineer. This tender scene illustrates a trainman's fond goodbye to his family.
Collection of the Library of Congress

RESTING COMFORTABLY after jumping aboard a gondola car in a rear-end collision, this Pennsy engine looks quite smug.

Chapter Six

Rear-End Collisions

As with head-on accidents in the previous chapter, rear-end collisions became a serious hazard to rail travelers after the Civil War. In 1882 an editorial in *Scientific American* described the danger quite dramatically: "Collisions, in fact, like the assassin's stab, are now more to be dreaded from the rear than from the front."

After 1865 America's railroads moved with enormous growth from their pioneer period of small, light trains into their mature era in which trains were long, heavy, and crowded with passengers. As traffic increased and it became necessary on heavily travelled roads to run many trains close together, the threat of rear-end collisions increased alarmingly. If the number of passengers on a scheduled run exceeded the capacity of one train, the company would often put an extra train on the one scheduled. In other words there were actually two trains for one that was scheduled. The second train would follow the first at a distance of a few hundred yards; the trains were within sight of each other, except when the first disappeared for a time around a curve.

The danger of rear-end collisions was slight as long as the speeds of the two-section trains was slow—fifteen to twenty miles per hour. Later on, after the War, when train speeds went up to 35 to 45 miles an hour, a very real danger from rear-end smashups arose. Clearly, the practice of operating a single train in sections presented a good many dangers, as it was difficult to coordinate the speeds and distances between the separate units running together. Often collisions resulted when the first unit slowed, stopped, or broke down. Also it must be remembered that trains were hard to stop in an emergency then as old fashioned hand brakes were still in use on most lines until the 1890's. Consequently, sections after 1870 usually ran five minutes apart, not within sight of each other. This time interval system nevertheless had inherent difficulties. How was the engineer of the following train to know that he was precisely five minutes behind the train ahead. Disasterous rear-end accidents occurred when the time interval between sections failed. In fact, rear-end collisions remained the single worst type of railroad accident for fifty years after 1870.

In the event of a breakdown or unscheduled stop of a train, a flagman was sent out to protect his train and to warn any approaching train of danger ahead. In the days before automatic signals, which came into use around 1880, flagging was any signal by use of

Timely Warning.

flags, lanterns, fuses, or torpedoes, used to warn an approaching train. Any delay in protecting a halted or disabled train could cause a disaster. Prompt flagging was essential. Inadequate protection by flagmen was, however, a sadly familiar cause of many rear-end collisions.

The most catastrophic rear-end collision before 1880 was the Revere, Massachusetts Disaster of August 26, 1871. This wreck holds a special place in railroad history. Although only thirty-two people were killed, the accident made an impression on the imaginations of mid-Victorian Americans. Revere is no doubt one of the best known American railroad disasters.

The accident happened on the Eastern Railroad on a Saturday evening when traffic was especially heavy from three weekend events: two large camp meetings (revivals) and a military muster. Because of the many travelers, 192 trains left the Eastern's Boston depot daily that weekend. The normal number was 152. The Eastern mainline ran north from Boston to Salem via Lynn, Massachusetts, and several branches ran along the North Shore.

On the dark evening of August 26, about 8:30 an express running at 30 miles an hour came up from behind on a slow moving local, which had just pulled onto the main line from a branch at Revere. At first the engineer of the express didn't see the train ahead. Then sud-

denly out of the dark he made out some lights ahead of him. A moment later his headlight caught the rear car of the local. Instantly the engineer of the express whistled for brakes, but the train had only primitive hand brakes, and they failed to hold on the slippery rails. With its speed reduced only slightly, the express rammed into the rear of the local. On impact the engine forced itself two-thirds of the way into the rear car, causing the steam pipes to burst, searing the trapped victims with live steam. Coals from the firebox mixed with the oil from the broken kerosene car lamps and burst into flames. The flames spread quickly in the tinder-dry wood coaches.

Half of the occupants of the rear car of the local were killed—either crushed to death by the impact or burned in the resulting fire. A hundred other passengers were seriously injured. The public was indignant over the accident. Meetings were held in Boston to condemn the railroad. Shouts of "deliberate murder" were common as emotions ran high in decorous Boston. Actually the Eastern Railroad was a hopelessly conservative company. Their equipment was antiquated. Nearly twenty years after the telegraph had been used on railroads, the Eastern managers refused to adopt the device for their dispatching. They were still dependent on the old time-interval system. Neither had the Eastern come to use the Westinghouse air brake. Ensuing lawsuits which nearly bankrupted the railroad were clearly the result of its inept, old fashioned management.

Another major rear-end collision happened at Spuyten Duyvil, within the corporate limits of New York City. A number of prominent New York State politicians were traveling from a meeting of the Legislature in Albany back to the city on the evening of January 13, 1882. They were riding in style in the fancy parlor cars of the *Atlantic Express* of the Hudson River Railroad, one of Commodore Vanderbilt's roads. Some of the politicians, their staffs, plus the omnipresent lobbyists were relaxing in the club car. Others gathered with State Senator Wagner in the leisure of his palatial private car the *Empire,* the next-to-last car of the train. Wagner, a rich businessman turned public servant, had made a fortune as the founder of the Wagner Sleeping Car Company. His cars were considered wonders of comfort and elegance.

The express moved swiftly down through the beautiful Hudson Valley. Then about 7:30

THIS LONG ISLAND RAILROAD LOCOMOTIVE hit the rear of a stalled freight, smashing the wooden box car to pieces. The wreck took place at Bay Shore, L. I., on July 10, 1909. *Collection of the Library of Congress*

in the evening at Spuyten Duyvil the train came to a sudden, startling stop. Someone, probably a drunk, had pulled the emergency cord, and the air brakes clamped automatically. After the train had stood there for about fifteen minutes, Sen. Wagner walked back to the rear car, the Wagner-built *Idlewild,* to inquire about the delay. Just at that moment the *Tarrytown Special* plowed into the halted train. The last two cars were telescoped, and fires broke out from the overturned coal stoves. Sen. Wagner and seven others were burned to cinders.

The cause of the accident was failure to protect the stalled train. The rear signalman, George Melius, was brought to trial on a charge of manslaughter for failing to flag the following train. In spite of a good deal of evidence against him, Melius was found not guilty by a very lenient jury.

A most recent serious rear-end collision oc-

curred on the Lackawanna Railroad on July 4, 1912. That day another doomed excursion train bound for a holiday at Niagara Falls had to stop because of a stalled freight near Corning, New York. A thin fog was creeping up from a nearby river as a flagman went back a half mile to protect his train. Automatic block signals also operated to protect the halted excursion during its sojourn. About a quarter of an hour after the halt, the rear flagman, Pat Lane, saw a passenger express come down on him fast. He waved and shouted madly, but the express tore by at sixty-five m.p.h. In another moment he heard it crash into the rear of the standing train. Thirty-nine passengers lost their lives and eighty-six were injured.

The old wooden coach at the rear of the train was totally destroyed. Although the next car was of steel construction, its vestibules and platforms were badly crushed at both ends. In fact, the damage done to this steel car contin-

MASSACHUSETTS.—RAILWAY DISASTER AT REVERE STATION, NEAR BOSTON.—THE BANGOR EXPRESS OVERTAKING THE BEVERLY ACCOMMODATION TRAIN, EVENING OF AUGUST 26TH ; CONFLAGRATION FROM THE KEROSENE LAMPS.—SKETCHED BY J. H. HYDE.

THE MOST INFAMOUS REAR-END COLLISION of all was the Revere, Mass. wreck of Aug. 26, 1871, where thirty-two people were killed, either crushed to death by the impact or burned in the resulting inferno.

ued well into the seating area. The third car from the rear, the wooden sleeping coach *Esthonia,* was telescoped two-thirds of its length by the steel car. Both cars then fell on their sides in a culvert. The *Esthonia* was so badly smashed up that the wreckage was burned on the site. The forward express car, totally wrecked in the crash, was carrying $500,000 in cash and $400,000 in negotiable bonds. Fortunately the treasure remained intact.

What caused the accident? Evidently the engineer of the rear train did not see the signals which told him to stop. Investigation found the signals in good working order. The guilty engineer, Milton Schroeder, had been employed by the Lackawanna for forty-two years; yet he disregarded the signals showing danger ahead. He must not have seen the signal at all. He of course testified that fog obscured the signal, but most witnesses said the fog was too light to cause any obstruction.

Rear-end collisions continue to occur today in 1968. On most heavily travelled lines there are automatic block signals to show the condition of the track ahead. Still, crews disregard or ignore these warnings. No matter how carefully automatic signal systems operate, there is enormous room for human error. In 1944 a rear-end collision killed fifty people when a train crew on the Southern Pacific Railroad disregarded their signals. Again in 1945 a signalman failed to protect his train on the Great Northern, and thirty-four passengers were killed. Thirty-four died at Coshocton, Ohio, in 1950 on the Pennsy in a rear-end collision caused by failure to protect a stalled train. That same year at Richmond Hill, Long Island, seventy-nine were killed in a rear-end smash-up on the Long Island Road. The list continues to show that the most frequent cause of major railroad accidents remains the simple disregard of signals.

THE ONCE HANDSOME PEMBROKE lies half hidden among debris after it struck a slow moving gravel train in the winter of 1891.

RAILROAD WRECKS made a profound impression on children. They clambered over this wrecked engine *Pembroke* as though it were a gigantic toy. This rear-end wreck happened in November of 1891 on the C & M Railroad.

IT SEEMS HIGHLY IMPROBABLE, but it did happen. The Chicago & Alton engine climbed right onto a freight car loaded with coal after ramming it from the rear.

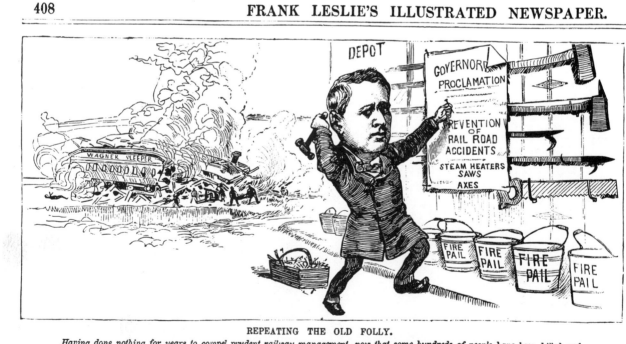

REPEATING THE OLD FOLLY.

Having done nothing for years to compel prudent railway management, now that some hundreds of people have been killed and injured, let us bolt and bar the door against disaster.

THE PENNSY'S *PENNSYLVANIA LTD.* was smacked from behind and pushed aside. Her cab was completely demolished by the impact. Such an accident cost the company thousands but local schoolboys thought it all great fun.

IN A BLINDING SNOWSTORM near Coburg, Ind. in 1886 these double-heading B & O engines smacked into the rear of another train. The men at the rear of the tender are carrying a fireman who was killed.

FRANK LESLIE'S
ILLUSTRATED
NEWSPAPER

Entered according to Act of Congress, in the year 1882, by Mrs. Frank Leslie, in the Office of the Librarian of Congress at Washington.— Entered at the Post Office, New York, N.Y., as Second-class Matter.

No. 1,375—Vol. LIII.   NEW YORK—FOR THE WEEK ENDING JANUARY 28, 1882.   [Price 10 Cents. $4.00 Yearly. 13 Weeks, $1.00

PRECAUTIONS AGAINST RAILROAD ACCIDENTS.—A LIGHTNING EXPRESS TRAIN STOPPED BY A TORPEDO ALARM.
See Page 398.

THE SHARP BLAST from a torpedo alarm signaled danger ahead to an engineer. Here a lightning express train is stopped by a torpedo just before colliding into the rear of a halted local.

FIVE PASSENGER COACHES were thrown off the track by the impact of this rear-end collision on the Pennsylvania Railroad near Pittsburgh. An injured passenger is shown being carried away from an overturned coach.

AT SIXTY-FIVE MILES AN HOUR a Lackawanna express crashed into the rear of a stalled excursion train near Corning, New York, on July 4, 1912, killing 39 people. This picture shows a steel car lying on its side and stripped of its trucks after telescoping the wooden sleeping car *Esthonia*, shown at the right. Scattered bedding is mute evidence of the sudden terror of the collision.

THIS GENERAL VIEW of the Corning, N.Y. wreck showing the terrible carnage that could result from a rear-end collision.

SEVERE TELESCOPING was typical in rear-end collisions. This one happened February 27, 1917, at Mt. Union, Pa., when a stalled Pennsylvania passenger train was struck from the rear by a fast freight. Twenty people were killed by the telescoping of the all steel sleeping car *Bellwood*.

ANOTHER VIEW of the telescoped pullmans in the Mt. Union disaster of 1917.

TWO PENNSY PASSENGER TRAINS tangled after an engineer ran through the signals and hit a stopped express right in front of the Tyrone, Pa. depot. The engine crushed the last car for a distance of twelve feet. The first postal car was thrown across the track and into the station. The engineer was killed; 150 passenger were injured in this wreck on July 30, 1913.

A ROCK ISLAND FREIGHT ENGINE was hit so hard from the rear by another engine that she was knocked completely off the track.

THIS BIG ILLINOIS CENTRAL STEAMER got her face smashed in when she butted into a freight train at Tinsley, Miss. on Jan. 31, 1941.

A Breakdown on the Road.

ANY BREAKDOWN OR UNSCHEDULED STOP presented a real threat of a rear-end accident. Disastrous wrecks occurred when flagmen were not quick to protect a halted or disabled train from an approaching locomotive.

UNITED STATES MAIL

PERSEVERANCE LINE.

WAY BILL,

From Philadelphia to Pittsburg.

March 29th 1838

FRANK LESLIE'S ILLUSTRATED NEWSPAPER.

THE FUTURE OF NEW ENGLAND RAILROADS.
Countryman—"Hello, stranger! Whar ye goin'?"   Traveler—"To Boston."
Countryman—"WHAT!!!"
Traveler—"Yes, I'll foot it. I don't want any White River or Forest Hills episodes in mine."

WHEN THE BOTTOM FELL OUT of this old truss bridge near Calvary, Ky., the engine, tender, and two cars of the Louisville & Nashville Road fell like flat irons into a dry creek bed. A lone coach teetered precariously atop a stone abutment.

84

Chapter Seven

Bridge Disasters

B<small>RIDGES ARE A PROBLEM</small>. They can fall down; flash floods can wash them away; a derailment on a bridge can cause a calamity; or a drawbridge can be left open in front of an approaching train. Very simply though, there are just three classes of railroad accidents brought about by the bridge itself: bridge collapses, washouts, and open drawbridges.

The first type of bridge accident facing the railroads, bridge collapse, is primarily a matter of engineering and construction. An amazing number of railroad bridges and trestles have fallen down under trains, especially during the nineteenth century. In 1887 alone there were twenty-one such bridge collapses. For one reason railroad bridges up to about the 1870's were usually built of wood. As timber was cheap, high, rickety trestles were built in place of more substantial metal or stone, and they weaved and groaned under the weight of trains. The railroad companies were economy minded, not very safety conscious, and wooden spans constructed along a variety of shoddy patterns were used because they were cheap and easy to build.

From 1840 until about 1870 the standard railroad bridge was the Howe truss, a rectangular trussed frame of wooden diagonals and vertical iron tie rods. This bridge was invented by William Howe, a farmer turned inventor. According to Lucius Beebe, the Howe truss was probably responsibile for as many railroad deaths as any other single cause. Although the engineering and construction of these truss bridges was probably not always the cause of their failure, there is no doubt that they were particularly vulnerable to floods, fire, and decay. They required constant inspection and repair. Also a number of bridge collapses can be traced to derailed trains striking the timber trusses and weakening the bridge enough to cause it to fall.

BRIDGE COLLAPSES

After 1870 the weights of both the locomotives and other rolling stock began to increase very rapidly. This change together with the development of the manufacture of iron beams gave a great impetus to the building of metal bridges. Even though iron bridges were designed to carry much heavier loads than wooden spans, they continued to collapse with frequency from structural failure during the nineteenth century. The infamous bridge collapse at Ashtabula in 1876 which killed eighty people was due to the

THE OLD WOODEN SPAN at Utica, N.Y. collapsed suddenly in May of 1858 under the weight of a crossing New York Central express bound for Cincinnati. Nine passengers were killed and fifty badly hurt as the coaches tumbled into the creek bed and broke apart like cheap furniture. Rescuers work to save the maimed and dying.

—Collection of the Library of Congress

failure of an all-iron Howe truss. Again in 1887 an iron bridge near Forest Hills, Massachusetts, fell under a train. The death toll there numbered twenty-four.

One memorable early bridge collapse dampened the spirits of the inaugural celebration for the Pacific Railroad. This bash, known as the Gasconade Bridge Disaster, occurred on the first of November 1855. A gay party of Pacific Railroad brass, politicians, and their ladies fell through the newly completed bridge over the Gasconade River, and twenty-two celebrities were drowned. Clearly, the iron-girder bridge was not ready to use. Because of the inevitable construction delays, the final span was not finished on opening day. The party crossed anyway—to their misfortune.

About three miles from Utica, New York, on the New York Central there used to be a forty-foot wooden bridge over Sauquoit Creek. On May 11, 1858, this bridge collapsed under the weight of two trains that passed on it, a passenger train and a freight. The eastbound Cincinnati Express was overwhelmingly destroyed, killing nine people and wounding fifty-five in the crunched cars. *Harpers Weekly*

reported this understatement: "Among the wounded, S. S. Horton of Binghamton, had his throat cut from ear to ear, as completely as though it had been done with a knife. It is said he will recover. A Mrs. Broderick was completely scalped, her head being quite circled as an Indian would do it . . ." What caused the bridge to fall? *Frank Leslie's Illustrated* said, "It was clearly proved that the bridge was more like punk than wood."

The Forest Hills Disaster shocked the entire country in the spring of 1887. The spectacle was a grim one. Dead from the wreck numbered twenty-four. The 125 others wounded suffered dreadfully. The first thing taken from the wreck was the headless body of a woman. Other victims were transfixed by splinters through the body. Some were crushed, some dismembered, and many mangled.

The train was a Boston-bound local going over the Dedham Branch of the Boston & Providence on a sunny Monday morning on March 14. There were about 300 people in the nine cars, mostly school children and commuters. About six miles from Boston the railway crosses Busey Bridge over a street near Forest Hills

ALL SIGNALS SAID GO, but the drawbridge wasn't there for this Rensselear & Saratoga passenger train. It crashed into the river at Troy, N. Y., in 1865.

Station. As this commuter train crossed Busey Bridge, the train fell like a cannon ball. The shock was so sudden and forceful that while the body of the fourth car fell, its roof, torn cleanly off, kept going straight ahead and landed on the embankment beyond the bridge. Another car turned over and fell on its roof, collapsing the sides like paper. Toward the rear of the train the cars fared little better. The splendid shape and symmetry of the moving train was replaced by a shapeless tangle of girders, trucks, rails, trusses, and smashed timbers. Inextricably tangled in the chaos were torn and bleeding bodies. For an instant there was silence, but as the victims collected their senses, there arose a most pitiable chorus of groans, shrieks, appeals, and commands. There was the usual hair-breadth escape. Two young men were pinned among the pile of inflammable debris. Just over their heads the car stove full of glowing coals hung menacingly. But the doors kept shut, and the bolts held firmly until they could be freed from the danger.

Though Busey Bridge was iron, it was poorly designed and of insufficient strength for the load it had to carry. Some time before the tragedy local residents had discovered loose nuts and bolts lying beneath it. Bridge designer Edmund Hewins was later exposed as a fraud. Also, the railroad had never bothered to inspect the fatal bridge.

WASHOUTS

The danger that railroads face from flash floods needs no explanation. In most parts of this country creeks, freshets, and runs can rise high during heavy rains. Raging flood waters can carry large trees and even houses down stream to pound against the foundations of railroad bridges and trestles. These washouts were quite devastating on the early roads because the bridges were flimsy then. In the days before iron spans, the destruction of smaller bridges by floods was commonplace. Hundreds of bridges had to be replaced annually after the spring floods.

Today, the danger of bridges being destroyed by wash-outs is especially prevalent in the West, where the rapid run-off in the semi-arid regions during heavy rainfall can transform a dry creek bed into a rushing sluiceway.

A flash flood caused a bad wreck on the Chicago, Burlington & Quincy in the fall of 1923, when a passenger train fell through a trestle bridge over Cole Creek near Lockett, Wyoming. Thirty-one passengers died after a surprise flooding of an ordinarily dry creek bed had weakened the supports of the bridge. Ironically, a bridge inspector, who had examined the span just an hour before the wreck, September 27, had reported it to be quite safe. Exactly what caused the sudden rise in the creek was never established, but it was believed that a sandbar holding back a large basin of water must have given way, releasing a sudden flood that hit the trestle just as the train started across at 9:15 p.m.

As the bridge fell in, the locomotive, tender, mail car, baggage car, smoker, and parlor car plunged into the flood. The first of the three sleeping cars was only partially submerged, and the last two remained on the track. Of the eighty people aboard, at least thirty-one lost their lives. Some of the bodies were buried in the mud of the creek, and others were swept far downstream by the swift current into the Platte River. Some of the cars were so deeply buried in the mud and sand that efforts to recover the bodies was impossible until the flood waters receded.

A B & O ENGINE AND TENDER lie upside down in the stream beneath the Carrolton Viaduct at Gwynn's Falls, Md. A side collision on the bridge on Aug. 13, 1900, sent them tumbling into the deep ravine.

WHEN THE BOSTON & ALBANY'S BRIDGE at Chester Mass., collapsed in 1907, the engine and half a dozen coaches rolled into a rocky stream bed.

Victorian reporters used to explain rail disasters from flash floods and wash-outs as "acts of God." Such explanations are rather ignorant. It seems obvious that the railroads could have anticipated the danger of flood and strengthened their bridges. They did not, nor have they to date.

OPEN DRAWS

There is yet another peril involving railroad bridges. That is the drawbridge. The railroads, realizing the special risk involved in using draw spans, were early to adopt various protective devices. Even so, numerous drawbridges have been left open in front of approaching trains. The major danger for trains at drawbridges is simply the engineer's disregard of all warning signals. Today the roads have gone to great lengths to reduce the risk of an open draw. Derailing devices are set automatically when the bridge is open. Nevertheless, drawbridge tragedies occur today on bridges equipped with the most modern safety features.

In the Disaster Year of 1853 there were two drawbridge accidents. The first was on April 23, when the Camden & Amboy's two o'clock train from Philadelphia ran off the draw into Rancocas Creek. The engineer didn't notice the signals and drove his train into the watery gorge. Fortunately, no one drowned.

Then came Norwalk. Within a few days after the Rancocas Creek accident, there occurred a second drawbridge calamity that was far and away the most disasterous railroad accident in American history at that time. Norwalk had the distinction of being the first of the great bridge disasters.

As the New Haven Road, which ran between New York and New Haven, was built as a shore line, it bridged a number of broad river estuaries emptying into Long Island Sound. One of these was a drawbridge over the Norwalk River at South Norwalk, Connecticut, about three hundred yards from the Norwalk depot around a sharp curve. Before the bridge tender opened this bridge for a ship, he would signal by lowering a red ball about the size of a basketball from a pole by the track.

At 10:15 on the morning of May 6, 1853, the steamboat *Pacific* whistled to pass the

89

WASHOUTS often caused rail travellers considerable delay in the early days. This New York Central bridge was swept completely away by a spring flood, leaving only the tracks dangling like wet strings. Passengers were forced to walk over an improvised footbridge to a waiting train on the other side that would carry them on their way.

Collection of the Library of Congress

closed bridge. Shortly after the steamer had passed through and as tender Harford was getting ready to close the bridge, he saw a Boston-bound passenger train speed around the curve and plunge into the river. The speed of the train carried the engine clear across the channel into the central pier of the bridge. A baggage car, two mail cars, and two passenger coaches fell into the river. A third coach teetered over the brink, then split in two. Forty-six lives were lost either by crushing or drowning. Feeling against the train crew, who had escaped by jumping from the doomed train, grew as an excited crowd gathered at the scene. Many people shouted that the engineer should be shot, but factions couldn't decide whether to hang him or shoot him. The coroner's inquest into the slaughter accused Engineer Tucker of gross negligence and held him primarily responsible for the tragedy.

America's most deadly drawbridge disaster stuck the Pennsylvania Railroad at Atlantic City, New Jersey, where the road crosses a deep tidal channel. On a Sunday afternoon, October 28, 1906, a brand new electrified train approached the bridge headed for the resort city and running at about forty miles an hour. Then suddenly the train careened off the rails at the entrance to the bridge, bumped over the ties for 150 feet, then veered off the bridge and plunged into deep water. The death toll was frightful—fifty-seven.

For fifty years the Atlantic City tragedy remained the last major railroad drawbridge accident. Then on the morning of September 15, 1958, a Jersey Central commuter train plunged over a high bridge spanning Newark Bay, and forty-eight city-bound commuters were instantly drowned. The draw was opened that morning to allow the small freighter *Sand*

Captain to pass through. Approaching the bridge from the Jersey Central main line came the commuter consisting of a double-unit diesel engine and five steel coaches. Although the draw span was fully protected by two automatic signals and an automatic derailing device, the train went through both signals without hesitating for a second, hit the derailing device at forty-two miles per hour, and skidded along the ties five hundred feet into the open draw. The engine and first two cars catapulted into the bay and instantly sank out of sight. The third coach, caught on the bridge by its rear trucks, hung suspended for about two hours; then it too fell into the deep water. The last two cars remained on the bridge. Since the engine, firemen, and conductor were all killed, the ICC investigators were not able to explain the cause of the clear disregard of signals.

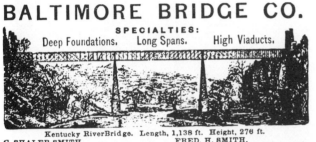
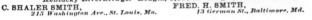
A CHAOTIC SCENE of wheels, rails, and parts strewn on top of the locomotive after a spring washout. A shoefly has been built around the wreckage so that traffic could be maintained.

EMPLOYES OF THE RAILWAY COMPANY RAISING THE LOCOMOTIVE FROM THE CHASM.

RHODE ISLAND.—SCENES AND INCIDENTS DURING AND AFTER THE TERRIBL' RAILWAY ACCIDENT NEAR RICHMOND SWITCH.—FROM SKETCHES BY JOS. BECKER.

SEARCHING FOR THE BODIES after the terrible washout at Wood River Jct., R.I. in 1873. Just before the accident, a dam upstream broke from heavy rains, letting water through in a terrific volume and carrying the bridge away. The train was going so fast when it reached the bridge that it jumped the chasm and struck the opposite bank as shown in the wood-cut. Following cars on the Stonington and Providence train were telescoped and set afire by overturned lamps and stoves. Nine passengers died in the wreck.

A FLASH FLOOD swept away the Rock Island Railroad bridge at Stratton, Colo., on July 18, 1929, scattering coaches into the swirling waters. When the flood receded, ten bodies were recovered.

THE HARTFORD LOCAL settled down in Camp Creek just outside of town after the bridge broke down. On the Saturday morning of June 12, 1882, a seven-car Hartford-bound train carrying many farmers and their families to their weekend tasks and errands in the city fell through a wooden bridge over Camp Creek. The engine, tender, and three wooden passenger cars fell into the shallow New England creek. The cause of the unfortunate plunge was a heavy spring rain the day before, which swelled the creek enough to weaken the unsturdy railroad bridge. When the local crossed the next morning, the supports gave way, and the train crashed through. The engineer and fireman were fatally injured in the wreck.

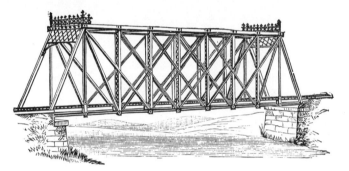

A FLIMSY WOODEN TRESTLE gave way under the weight of a crossing train and collapsed in the early summer of 1881 at Sunbury, Ohio.

Collection of the Library of Congress

A SPRING FRESHET near Cincinnati washed out the iron truss bridge on the Indianapolis & St. Louis Road at Hillsboro, Ohio in 1893.

THE DISASTER AT BUSSEY BRIDGE, NEAR FOREST HILLS, ON THE BOSTON AND PROVIDENCE RAILROAD.—Drawn by Henry Sandham.

THE BUSSEY RIDGE DISASTER at Forest Hills, Mass. shocked the nation in 1887. Twenty-four people died when an iron bridge fell.

A DELICATE BALANCE saved the passengers in this car from death. On Oct. 17, 1884, the railroad bridge over the Little Miami River at Batavia, Ohio, collapsed under the weight of this train. The engine, baggage car and first coach fell fifty feet into the river. The last coach was very lucky.

A MARVELLOUS ESCAPE—THE RAILWAY ACCIDENT AT BATAVIA, OHIO.—From a Photograph by John A. Kline.—[See Page 725.]

A DERAILMENT ON A BRIDGE of the St. Lawrence & Adirondack Railroad about 1917 drew a crowd of curious onlookers.

HER SISTER ON THE GROUND the Baltimore & Lehigh narrow gauge No. 6 hangs precariously but safe derailed on the trestle at Vale, Md. in the early winter of 1899.

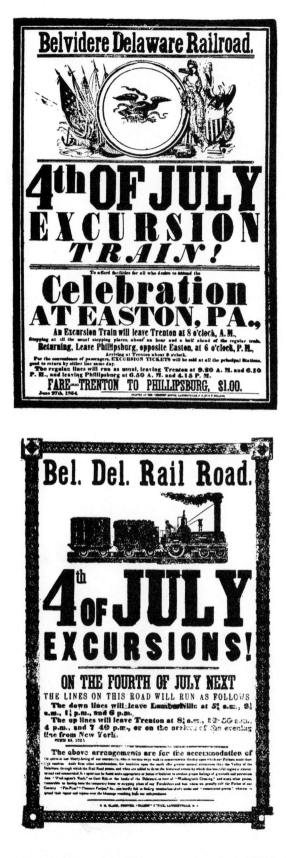

A LEHIGH VALLEY TRAIN of fourteen wooden coaches filled with Union veterans and their families returning from a GAR reunion was derailed at Rochester, N.Y., on Aug. 25, 1911, by a broken rail. Unfortunately, the derailment occurred at a bridge over the Canandaigua, and two of the cars plunged forty feet into the stream bed, killing 28 passengers. The disaster drew crowds, some of whom posed gaily aside the fatal wreckage. Others watched as bodies of victims were lined up in a makeshift morgue.

A SURPRISE FLOOD of an ordinarliy dry creek at Lockett, Wyo., on Sept. 27, 1923, brought disaster to this Chicago, Burlington & Quincy train. Several cars were totally submerged in the swift current after the bridge gave way. Twenty-two passengers lost their lives.

ANOTHER WASHOUT on the Fort Worth & Denver Railroad in 1918 sent this freight engine headlong into a mudbank. The engineer's body (see the arrow) is trapped in the wreckage. The washout completely eroded the foundations on either side of the concrete culvert.

Collection of the Library of Congress

SPRING THAWS were a constant hazard to railroads. The melting snow in the Rockies near Eddy, Montana washed out the tracks of the Northern Pacific Railroad, sending the coaches tumbling down the river bank.

Collection of the Library of Congress

AMERICA'S MOST DEADLY DRAWBRIDGE ACCIDENT struck the Pennsylvania Railroad at Atlantic City, New Jersey on Oct. 28, 1906. Fifty-seven were drowned. Here one of the fatal electric cars is being hauled out of the deep water.

THE SIGNAL SAID ALL CLEAR as the train approached the bridge but the draw was open and the engine plunged into the void. Notice the red signal ball in lowered position at the right.

THE NEWARK BAY DRAWBRIDGE DISASTER of Sept. 15, 1958, was one of the worst tragedies of recent years. Forty-eight New York bound commuters were drowned instantly when a Jersey Central electric ran through an open draw. One coach hung precariously for two hours before plunging into the bay.

ONE OF THE MOST DISASTROUS telescope accidents of all was the one at Mud Run, Pa., Oct. 10, 1888. Sixty-four people on an excursion of the Total Abstinence Union were killed in the gruesome telescope of these rickety Lehigh Valley Railroad carriages. The train had stopped briefly at Mud Run when it was rammed from behind by a speeding express.

Chapter Eight

Telescopes

Passenger cars telescoped with horrible frequency in the nineteenth century. In a head-on or rear-end collision, or derailment the fatalities usually stemmed from telescoping of the flimsy wooden coaches. The word *telescoping* is used by railroad men to explain the kind of accident in which one car forces its way into another car.

If the impact from either the front or rear were great enough, one car could be driven against another with sufficient force to pentrate, or telescope it. In a collision one coach would be thrust into the car ahead, sweeping away the studding and wood bracing, and crushing the stoves, seats, and passengers, until, if the momentum was great enough, several cars would be enclosed in each other like the tubes in a partially shut telescope.

Telescoping of passenger cars, figuring as it did in almost all of the great wrecks, was premier among the horrors of rail travel. At Camp Hill, Revere, Chatsworth, Secaucus, and Silver Creek, to list only a few—in all of these wrecks telescoping was the greatest killer. Charles Francis Adams, railroad accident authority and Railroad Commissioner for Massachusetts, stated that at least half of the deaths and injuries in rail accidents in his time were caused by the telescoping of passenger cars.

One of the most disastrous telescope accidents was Mud Run. On October 10, 1888, the Total Abstinence Union held a huge rally in the Pennsylvania mountains at Hazelton. Eight excursion trains hauled 5,000 people over the Lehigh Valley Railroad from Wilkes-Barre. Because of the heavy traffic on the line Superintendent Mitchell issued orders that trains running in sections must keep ten minutes apart. Also trains were cautioned to protect their rears as a special safety precaution. As the temperance specials returned toward Wilkes-Barre after the day's outing, the sixth train stopped at about eight o'clock at Mud Run Pennsylvania along the bank of the Lehigh River. The 500 passengers on board were still in high spirits. Newspaper reports indicate that not all of the revellers had been totally abstemious in spite of the occasion. The train had not been standing long when another section came along and plowed twenty feet into the last car of the halted train. The collision caused the last car to tesescope half of the car ahead of it. Of the two hundred people in these two cars, sixty-four were killed outright. A hundred others were injured.

TELESCOPING is a type of railroad accident in which one car forces itself inside another car like the tubes in a partially closed telescope. In such accidents passengers were usually crushed to death from the force. This Old Colony Railroad engine has completely telescoped a wooden coach. The shell of the coach rests over the engine in a deadly masquerade.

A commemorative book called the *First Anniversary of the Mud Run Disaster* by Matt. J. Meredith, records a bit of the antique gore of the disaster: "Oh! What tongue can tell, or what pen picture this most dreadful calamity. The roasting, scalding engine under which were crushed those poor young children, and the car ahead being telescoped and the lives crushed out of those who but a few moments since were full of life. Oh, God, why visit upon your unhappy children such a death."

The cause of the many telescope accidents was due directly to the American system of passenger car construction and train coupling. The link and pin coupling became the standard method of linking cars together after about 1840, but unfortunately it did not hold the cars very close together. As a result the car platforms were able to bounce up and down, greatly increasing the danger of telescoping. In England, where cars were coupled together with powerful compression, telescopes were rare. Another problem of this standard link and pin coupling was that it was attached to the car below the sills (or floors), so that the line of resistance was not the line of greatest strength. When the train stopped quickly, cars

pushed against each other at different levels.

In an accident one car could crash against another so violently that the bodies of the cars were likely to be broken and the cars pass into and sometimes through each other like the joints of a telescope. A remedy for the frequent telescopes of cars was not found until 1869 when the Miller Platform and Buffer was introduced. This device locked the ends of the car sills together and held them tightly by a strong tension-compression coupling. The cars joined in this way into a single platform couldn't rise above another to cause telescoping. The Miller invention was a great improvement in safety and comfort for the passenger, for in addition to reducing the threat of telescoping, it stopped the uncomfortable jerks in starting and stopping and made the whole train much more unified and steady.

The *New York Times* of February 12, 1873, contained an editorial endorsing Col. Miller's new platform: "The usefulness of this invention was again demonstrated on Monday last, when a Hudson River express train ran off the track near Coxsackie. The cars were provided with the patent coupler and platform (Miller's) and, as a consequence, the telescoping,

104

which otherwise would have been inevitable, did not occur. Had the cars of the express been coupled in the old-fashioned way, we should have had to chronicle a terrible loss of life."

After Miller's improvement of car platforms and couplers, it only remained necessary to perfect the construction of the passenger car to insure safety. Although Miller's patent was not universally adopted by all roads, the principles of his invention were sound enough to force themselves into general acceptance as other men marketed buffer-couplers designed along the same lines.

The second principal cause of telescoping was the American system of car building. The wooden passenger car which prevailed throughout the nineteenth century was not strong enough to stand up in a wreck and was easily telescoped. With the abundance of timber available in this country, wooden cars were cheap to build but not very sturdy. In collisions they were quickly turned into heaps of expensive kindling or flew apart like smashed packing cases. In the event of a telescope the passengers riding inside had no protection because the thin wooden walls offered little resistance from crushing.

There was a constant demand for better accommodations on passenger trains, and by the early 1840's companies began paying a good deal of attention to style, interior decoration, fittings, and comfort in their cars. Soon cars

WOODEN PASSENGER CARS were popular throughout the nineteenth century because they were cheap and easy to build. However, they were not very sturdy. In a collision the thin wooden walls offered passengers inside little protection from being crushed to death from telescoping. This car is in the B & O Railroad Museum in Baltimore.

seating fifty people were running on the major lines. Some coaches even had elegant ladies' compartments with hand-carved woodwork, fine mirrors, and seats upholstered in red velvet plush. Nevertheless, these lavished furnished cars were still made of wood and were not a bit safer than any ordinary wooden car. Although there was some interest in metal cars, wood was the standard material for coaches in America until the turn of the century.

The best known of the early metal cars was the LaMothe Car, patented by Dr. Bernard J. LaMothe in 1854. The metal frame was built like a cage of elastic steel bars. The great advantage claimed for this over the ordinary wooden car was its resistance to telescoping and breaking apart in case of an accident. To protect the passengers further, the car was lined throughout with soft padded upholstery. A few of the LaMothes were actually built and used on eastern roads, but metal cars were only considered a novelty by railroad companies for some time to come.

By the 1870's and 1880's cars had reached such a great size and weight that car builders began to search for some method to make them stronger. By 1875 steel was being used in repairing wrecked coaches. The next step, of course, was that steel bracing was being substituted for wood in new cars in areas where great strength was required. Still, as the cars were basically wood, these steel-braced cars were not much stronger. The evolution of the all-metal car was slow but inevitable. After all steel cars were first built for the New York City subway in 1904, the idea caught on rapidly with other roads. In a couple of years several railroads had steel cars in service, and car builders could furnish any number of coach designs in steel.

Unfortunately many roads made slow progress in adopting steel cars. Even after the grim warning of the New York, New Haven

FRANTIC RESCUE WORK at Jackson, Michigan, after a crash on the Michigan Central road, October 1879. Eighteen passengers, mostly emigrants, were killed in the frightful telescope of the first coach.

Collection of the Library of Congress

HEAVILY VARNISHED WOODWORK, linoleum ceilings, velvet seats, oil lamps, and the cast iron coal stove (visible at right center) added to the combustible nature of the wooden passenger car.

and Hartford's Stamford collision of 1913, which killed six passengers in a splintering telescope, New Haven Vice President in charge of operations, Horn, stated that he was doubtful about the desirability of steel cars compared to wooden ones. He told the ICC that he would have to be convinced. As late as 1913 the New Haven had 2,257 wooden cars and only 30 steel.

Ironically, the first steel coaches were dis-guised to look as though they were wood. Manufacturers went to great pains to imitate the elaborate finish of the old wood cars by painting the steel plates to simulate mahogany and parquetry. Custom and tradition are very powerful forces even in shaping our technology.

There can be no doubt that the all steel passenger car made rail travel infinitely safer than ever before. It would, however, be naive to assume that metal alone could prevent tele-

MILLER'S
TRUSSED PLATFORMS, COMPRESSION BUFFERS
AND
Automatic Couplers,
FOR
RAILROAD PASSENGER CARS.

Office, 231 Broadway (Rooms 4 & 5).

DESCRIPTION.

Figure 1 is an elevation; figure 2, a longitudinal section: figure 3, a plan of an end of a car to which the arrangement has been applied; and figures 4 and 5 show top and side views of the "Hook" and "Buffer," drawn on a larger scale than that of figures 1, 2 and 3.

The letters refer to the same parts in all the figures. A is the coupling "Hook;" B the "Buffer;" C the "Stop;" D the "Lever;" E the "Quadrant Rachet;" F the "Truss Beam;" G the "Spring Beam;" H the "Suspender Beam;" I the "Upward Trusses;" K the "Main Spring;" L the "Downward Trusses," and M the "Bolster."

The platforms, instead of being located below the centre line of the main sills of the cars, are placed *in* that line, and held there by the Trusses I and L, so that the point of contact (in Buffer B) *is* in the said centre line and *not below it.* The coupling "Hook" A is attached to the draw spring the same as the ordinary draw head, and at the same height above the track, but in such a manner that the outer end is free to move laterally for a short distance. The Coupling Hook projects beyond the platform. The Stop C is placed under the Buffer Beam to prevent accidental uncoupling. When two cars are brought together, the Coupling Hooks, from *their shape,* push each other aside, until the Buffers B are compressed hard on the Buffer Springs, then—*the points of the Hooks having passed each other sufficiently far*—the Hooks are carried forward by their main-springs, and thus the "Coupling" and "Compression" are both effected automatically *and at the same time,* and without the use of links and pins. When two cars are thus coupled together, the *head of the Hook* of each car is under the Buffer Beam of its opposite car, and the platforms are close together (about 4 inches apart). The effect of this is, *one platform cannot be forced over the other* nor can a *child* fall between the platforms; the dust and rain are nearly all shut out; the "Compression" makes the train run steadily, and prevents all jerking at starting and stopping. In short, the advantages gained by the use of these improvements may be summed up briefly, as follows:

1. The platforms are held in a plane with the sills of the cars. 2. The platforms cannot be broken by any ordinary accident. 3. *Telescoping* is entirely prevented. 3. Any required compression may be attained, to prevent accidents by *Oscillation.* 5. No links and pins are required. 6. The platforms may be held as closely together as desired. 7. By close coupling the train is shortened. 8. They will not accidentally uncouple. 9. They may be uncoupled "without shutting off" to make a *flying switch.* 10. They very much reduce lateral and vertical unsteadiness of the cars. 11. They cause the train to move steadily and not jerk in starting and stopping. 12. They work well at great variations of height. 13. They will couple with all kinds of "drawheads" and "couplers." 14. They are cheap and durable. 15. Injury to men when coupling cars is entirely prevented. 16. Injury to persons by falling between cars is entirely prevented. 17. Injury to persons and to cars by "telescoping" is entirely prevented. 18. Injury to persons and to cars by "oscillation" is entirely prevented. 19. The great steadiness of the cars—*produced by compression*—renders sleeping-cars much more desirable. 20. *Train Brakes* are rendered more valuable by the non-existence of "slack" in the train.

A **REMEDY** for the frequent telescope accidents was not found until 1869 when Ezra Miller patented his successful platform and buffer. The Miller Platform, which locked the cars together by strong compression, was a great improvement in safety because it reduced the threat of telescoping.

scoping of cars. The potential for disaster did in fact keep pace with progress. As steel construction and heavier trucks came into use, so did the speeds of trains accelerate to ninety and a hundred miles per hour. Accidents occurring after 1905 were quite as frightful as ever before. On February 27, 1917, at Mt. Union, Pennsylvania, a rear-end collision caused the telescoping of an all steel car, killing every person inside.

There was a dense fog as the Pennsylvania Railroad's *Mercantile Express* and eight steel cars stopped at the Mt. Union station after discharging passengers. The train was momenta-rily unable to proceed because the brakes on the first mail car had stuck. As the fireman was attempting to release the brakes, the train was struck from the rear by a fast freight running at forty-one miles an hour. The force of the collision caused a disasterous telescope of the rear car, the sleeping car *Bellwood,* by the Pullman *Bruceville.* The sleeping car was telescoped its entire length, and all of the nineteen passengers and the porter were killed. The whole train was pushed two hundred feet ahead by the collision, and several cars of the freight derailed and fell down an embankment.

Although all the cars on the express were

of all steel construction, the structure was obviously faulty as it possessed little strength against telescoping. The sill of the *Bruceville* was raised above that of the *Bellwood,* and the force stripped the superstructure of the last car, leaving it a flat car.

It is not to be expected that any passenger car can be built to resist all kinds of shocks. Obviously any car can be destroyed, depending entirely on the nature of the accident. Still, with the advances in coupling, buffering, heating, and steel construction, the standard American passenger coach has evolved into a safe, robust structure capable of withstanding tremendous impacts.

A DERAILED LOCOMOTIVE has slashed deeply into this wooden car, leaving it a pile of worthless kindling.

THIS BALTIMORE & OHIO EXPRESS CAR was wrecked in 1918 at Reduction, Pa., when a locomotive was derailed by a brake beam falling to the track. Two men lost their lives by the telescoping of this wooden car.

THE IMPACT FROM A HEAD-ON COLLISION produced this fierce telescope of a baggage car on the Grand Rapids and Indiana Road. The light construction of the car offered little resistance to telescoping. The end and floor have been cleanly stripped away.

TELESCOPING OF PASSENGER CARS caused great loss of life in 1886 when a Nickle Plate excursion train headed for Niagara Falls rammed a freight near Silver Creek, N.Y. Twenty men were crushed to jelly in the smoking car.

FRANK LESLIE'S ILLUSTRATED NEWSPAPER.

89

SEPTEMBER 25, 1886.]

1. EXTRICATING THE DEAD AND WOUNDED.   2. WRECK OF THE LOCOMOTIVES AND FREIGHT TRAIN.

NEW YORK.—COLLISION OF AN EXCURSION TRAIN WITH A FREIGHT TRAIN ON THE NEW YORK, CHICAGO AND ST. LOUIS ("NICKEL PLATE") RAILROAD, NEAR SILVER CREEK, ON TUESDAY, THE 14th INST.—NINETEEN LIVES LOST.

FROM SKETCHES BY R. LE BARRE GOODWIN.—SEE PAGE 93.

TELESCOPING OF PASSENGER CARS, figuring as it did in almost all of the great wrecks, was premier among the horrors of travel. At Chatsworth, Ill., on Aug. 10, 1887, a Toledo, Peoria & Western excursion bound for Niagara Falls fell through a small trestle. Nine coaches tumbled into a pile, and eighty-two passengers were killed in a dreadful telescope of cars.

ANOTHER VIEW of the splintered wreckage of coaches at the Chatsworth wreck.

SOME OF THE FIRST STEEL COACHES were disguised to look as though they were wooden. Metal plates were painted to simulate mahogany such as on this sideswiped parlor car.

STEEL CAR CONSTRUCTION undoubtedly made rail travel safer than before. Nevertheless, metal alone did not prevent the telescoping of cars. The potential for death and destruction did keep up with progress, as illustrated by these shots of a steel coach that was telescoped in a rear collision in Philadelphia in 1924.

EVEN AFTER THE COMPANIES BEGAN TO BUILD STEEL CARS about 1907, dreadful telescopes continue to scar rail safety. On Feb. 27, 1917, at Mt. Union, Pa., a rear-end collision caused the telescoping of an all steel car, killing every person inside.

ANOTHER EXAMPLE of the vulnerability of steel cars to telescoping is this mangled coach of the Northern Pacific Road, which was crushed a third its length in 1913 at Lakeview, Wash.

A REAR-END COLLISION at Tyrone Pa. on July 30, 1913 threw this Pennsylvania Railroad postal car diagonally across the track, the front end striking the station and coming to rest on the station platform. Because of its steel construction, most of the shock of the collision was absorbed by the platform and vestibule of the cars. No passengers were killed.

THE HEAVY STEEL REINFORCEMENT of these NYC cars prevented crushing to extend past the vestibules when the train stopped short from a boiler explosion on July 27, 1928, at Bergen, N.Y.

FRANK LESLIE'S ILLUSTRATED NEWSPAPER

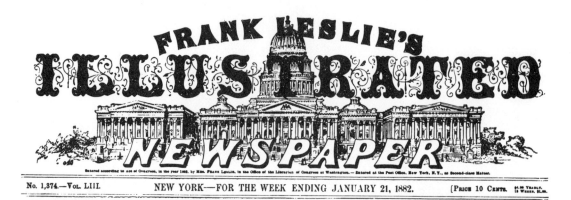

Entered according to Act of Congress, in the year 1882, by Mrs. Frank Leslie, in the Office of the Librarian of Congress at Washington. — Entered at the Post Office, New York, N.Y., as Second-class Matter.

No. 1,374.—Vol. LIII.   NEW YORK—FOR THE WEEK ENDING JANUARY 21, 1882.   [Price 10 Cents. $4.00 Yearly. 12 Weeks, $1.00.

NEW YORK.—THE FATAL COLLISION ON THE HUDSON RIVER RAILROAD, NEAR SPUYTEN DUYVIL, JANUARY 13TH.

IN THE ABSENCE OF FIRE FIGHTING EQUIPMENT, trainmen, passengers, and men from nearby farmhouses used huge snowballs to combat the flames of Spuyten Duyvil, N.Y. collision of 1882. The Hudson River road's *Tarrytown Special* plowed into the rear of the halted *Atlantic Express*, telescoping the last two coaches and setting fire to the wreckage. Eight prominent politicians were burned to cinders.

118

Chapter Nine

Fires

THE SYSTEM OF HEATING used in American passenger trains was clearly an invention of the devil. The cause of some of the worst disasters was the primitive car stove. The possibility for holocaust inherent in a red-hot cannonball stove in each passenger coach that might go into a ditch was enormous.

In any derailment or collision the potbellied stove was certain to tip over, spilling out red-hot coals and cinders onto the passengers and about the car. The tinder dry wooden cars then quickly burst into raging fire that burned many a trapped or injured passenger to a crisp. Because of the "deadly car stove," many minor accidents were turned into fiery disasters. Wrecks with the longest casualty lists were almost invariably accompanied by fires from overturned stoves: Camp Hill, Angola, Revere, Ashtabula, Spuyten Duyvil.

From the earliest days of railroading everyone realized the great danger of fire from the stoves in case of accident, and various attempts were made to heat the cars by other means. Ways were suggested of conveying hot air from the locomotive to the coaches, but it was difficult to make a flexible air duct between the cars, and there was danger of fire from an overheated duct. Another method was devised to circulate hot water through pipes in the floors of the cars. Actually, there were countless car heaters patented to eliminate the danger of fire. Most of them were worthless; in 1868 a hot water heater was introduced, but the water was heated by a coal fire. It was not until steam from the engine boiler was used in 1887 that the heating system was truly safe.

Although steam had been considered for car heating as early as the 1860's, the danger of scalding the passengers was as great as the peril of fire from the stoves. This problem was finally overcome by the invention of a valve that reduced the boiler steam to a pressure safe enough to use in the cars. Steam was first used to heat an entire train in the winter of 1887, and soon afterward it came into general use.

Fires in wrecked trains have also started quite often from kerosene lamps as well as from the coal stoves. In their state of infancy, railroads seldom ran night trains; when they did, travel was a dark and gloomy business. Until 1840 cars were lighted by candles. As the Pullman cars grew in elegance, kerosene lamps replaced candles in the 1860's. These coal-oil lamps were brighter than candles but also more dangerous, as

119

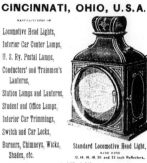

THE ANGOLA DISASTER—THE BURNING CAR.—[Sketched by J. P. Hoffman.]

they could spray liquid fire in case of a wreck. Therefore, various systems were introduced using compressed coal gas for illumination. Of these the Pintsch gaslight was the best as it was quite safe. In 1882 the Pennsylvania Railroad tried lighting cars with electricity. By 1887 whole trains were being illuminated by electric lamps, thus greatly reducing the danger of fire from smashed lamps in an accident.

FORTY-TWO PEOPLE were burned to cinders in the bridge derailment at Angola, N.Y., in 1867. Broken stoves scattered coals everywhere, and the brightly varnished coaches soon became incinerators.

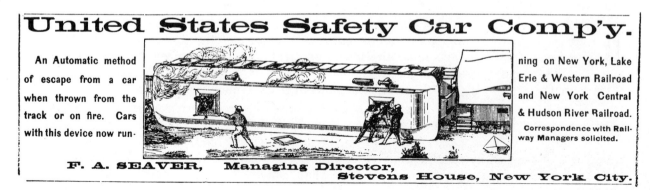

A FEW MINUTES AFTER THE IMPACT of a rear end collision, kerosene from the engine *Franklin*'s headlamp ignited, turning the telescoped rear sleeping car into a blazing torch. When the fire finally burned itself out, all of the cars of the *Lightning Express* were reduced to smoldering, charred ruin. This firey disaster occurred just north of Cincinnati on the C. H. & D. (now the B & O) on Nov. 21, 1867.

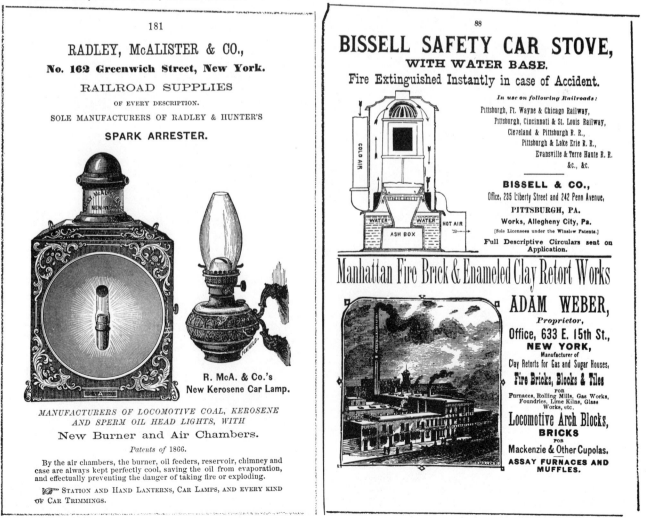

FRANK LESLIE'S
ILLUSTRATED
NEWSPAPER

Entered according to Act of Congress, in the year 1887, by Mrs. Frank Leslie, in the Office of the Librarian of Congress at Washington.— Entered at the Post Office, New York, N.Y., as Second-class Matter.

No. 1,635.—VOL. LXIII.]   NEW YORK—FOR THE WEEK ENDING JANUARY 15, 1887.   [PRICE, 10 CENTS. $4.00 YEARLY. 13 WEEKS, $1.00.

OHIO.—THE RECENT TERRIBLE RAILROAD DISASTER NEAR REPUBLIC—SEARCHING THE RUINS OF THE WRECK FOR THE BODIES OF VICTIMS.

FROM A PHOTOGRAPH BY C. D. SPRAGUE.—SEE PAGE 374.

EARLY IN THE MORNING of Jan. 4, 1887, at Republic, Ohio, a westbound Baltimore and Ohio express travelling at 65 miles and hour crashed head-on into an eastbound freight. The wreck quickly caught fire; thirteen passengers died.

DERAILMENT OF STEAM-HEATED CARS AT FREDONIA, N. Y.

THESE CARS ON THE DUNKIRK, ALLEGHENY VALLEY & PITTSBURGH ROAD were saved from probable fire when they derailed in 1887 because they were equipped with a new kind of car heater—steam heat in place of stoves. It was about this time that most of the more prosperous companies were getting rid of the dangerous coal stove.

124

WINSLOW'S
Improved Safety Car Heater and Ventilator.

A Perfect Safeguard against Fire in case of Accident. The Strongest and most Durable Stove made. The most Economical, on account of the very large volume of air heated. Their use insures Health, Safety and Comfort.

We claim for our Heaters the following advantages over any other in use for Railway Cars:

An equal quantity of hot air is distributed throughout the car.

Persons sitting near the stove are not hotter than those at a distance, and are not obliged to open the windows to the annoyance of others.

We require only one opening for pipe through the roof, a benefit car-builders will readily understand.

They are the strongest and most durable Heater made.

No steam pipes to get out of order, to require cars to be sent to shop for repairs.

The heat can be perfectly regulated for mild or very cold weather.

No. 3.

We claim for our Heaters the following advantages over any other in use for Railway cars:

All the impure air is driven out at the top of the car.

The air in the car never comes in contact with the heated surface of the stove, as all the air that is heated is brought fresh from the outside—thus heating and ventilating the car at the same time

There is no danger of accidents from passengers' clothing taking fire by coming in contact with the stove.

In numerous cases where cars containing this stove have been overturned, it has never been known to set fire to the car.

We invite special attention to the above cut, which illustrates **Winslow's Improved Safety** Car Heater and Ventilator. Many devices have been tried for heating and ventilating railway cars, and most of them have proven failures ; but by our improved plan cars can be thoroughly heated and ventilated. The fresh air is taken in at the top of the car through the ventilator, passing down a pipe around the smoke pipe to the top of the stove, and around the heated cylinder and through an iron elbow into a 4x6 air box along the side of the car, through registers between the seats, thus warming the feet of passengers, thoroughly heating the car, and forcing the foul air out through the top openings ; thus constantly changing the air in the car. Persons who travel in railway cars know how uncomfortably hot the seats near the stove are, and how often they are obliged to open the windows, to the annoyance of passengers at a distance from the stove, who are suffering from the cold ; and also how *illy ventilated* most cars are, on account of the air coming in contact with the heated steam pipes or plates of stoves. They are also a splendid ventilator in a car for summer use. Six years' successful use of them, and many of the leading railroads having adopted them for their standard Heaters, prove their superiority over all others. The price of above Heater, with hot-air elbow, is forty dollars net each, free on cars here.

A. P. WINSLOW & CO., Manufacturers, CLEVELAND, O.

W. D. DRAKE, General Agent, Cleveland, O.

AN INCIDENT OF RAILROAD TRAVEL—A HOT BOX.—[Drawn by Thomas Worth.]

A HOT-BOX HAS HALTED A CROWDED TRAIN; passengers, who accepted such delays as inevitable, watch while a train-man repacks the over-heated bearing.

Chapter Ten

Running Gear Failure: "Hotboxes" and Broken Parts

"A MOST MELANCHOLY ACCIDENT occurred on the Columbia railroad, on Saturday afternoon, Oct. 2 [1836]. In the forward passenger car was a number of persons; among others, Mrs. Gibson and family, of Philadelphia bound for Cincinnati. The axle of the car unfortunately broke, and let the body down upon the road, by which a large hole was forced through the car, and Mrs. Gibson and child, by some means, were dragged through to the ground, and nearly the whole train passed over her body, crushing it in a most shocking manner, and leaving her a lifeless corpse. The child miraculously escaped death, ..." This rather stoic account of an early accident caused by a broken axle appeared in Howland's *Steamboat Disasters and Railroad Accidents in the United States*, which overlays the most lurid calamity with antique charm.

Broken wheels and axles were a prolific cause of rail wrecks in the first three or four decades of railroad travel in America. Still today, in spite of the improved metals of locomotive and car wheels, these parts are subject to such extreme pressures and torsions that they can fracture and break under stress, bringing about immediate wreckage. In the past, when wheels were manufactured from inferior cast iron, accident from broken wheels were common. Later on, about 1865, steel tires were put on locomotive wheels to avoid the breakage of the cast iron wheels. Steel tires had the advantage that when they became worn, their treads and flanges could be replaced.

A broken axle was the cause of the first fatal railroad accident in America — the 1833 crash on the Camden & Amboy discussed in Chapter I. Also the "Angola Horror" of 1867 (See Chapt. 3), probably the country's most notorious railroad disaster, was caused by a defective axle.

Equally as dangerous as a broken axle or wheel is the overheated wheel journal, commonly known as the "hotbox." The "hotbox" was always a great nuisance to early rail travelers. Many times the trouble was spotted before a derailment occurred, and the traveller had only to put up with the delay while the journal was fixed. The train would be halted in order to extinguish the flames from the overheated box, and more often than not the delay was not accompanied by mishap. To eliminate the problem of "hotboxes," many railroads are presently converting to the more costly roller bearings.

Although the cost of conversion to roller bearings is great, it would seem that safety would require the managers to adopt them on all passenger service. One fatal "hotbox" accident happened on a sunny autumn afternoon on September 6, 1943. The Pennsylvania's *Congressional Ltd.*, on the way from Washington City to New York, went around a curve outside of Philadelphia and without warning lurched off the track. The seventh car was thrust almost vertically into the air, striking the frame of a signal bridge which ripped savagely through the entire length of the car. Seven following cars also left the rails and were strewn wildly over the main line tracks. Eighty passengers in the heavily loaded train were killed. The cause of the wreck was an overheated journal, which broke an axle and derailed the cars. The wreck at Philadelphia was the greatest "hotbox" disaster in American history.

A DYING BEHEMOTH: A broken axle toppled this handsome engine of the Natalbany Lumber Company at Yawn, La. on June 4, 1937.

ON CHRISTMAS EVE 1872 a dreadful derailment took place at Prospect Station, Pa. Twenty-five passengers were killed when coaches fell from the bridge into a frozen creek bed, where they were set afire from overturned stoves. The derailment was caused by a broken wheel.

THE RAILROAD ACCIDENT AT PROSPECT STATION, PENNSYLVANIA.—From a Sketch by E. Y. Breck.—[See Page 61.]

PASSENGER COACHES OF THE SOUTHERN PACIFIC MORNING EXPRESS lie scattered over the roadbed at Deady, Ore. The derailment was caused when an engine driving wheel broke at high speed in 1928.

RUNNING DEEP IN BOULDER CANYON, this little Colorado Central narrow gauge broke a flange on an engine wheel and upset in a rushing mountain stream on April 4, 1893.

A BROKEN SIDE ROD swiped clean the engineer's side of the cab on this Deleware & Hudson engine This ever present danger to the engineer explains the eventual outlawing of "Mother Hubbard" locomotives.

THIS CENTRAL OF NEW JERSEY 583 was another "Mother Hubbard," or center cab engine, that broke a side rod; the ends of the rod are intact on the wheel pins; the center part of the rod broke loose and ravaged the cab.

ALL SAFE: The crew managed to stop the B & O's crack National Ltd. without incident after a rear driving wheel tire worked loose. Such tires were shrunk on to the wheel centers; no bolts or rivets were used to hold them in place. In a close-up shot, the engineer stands calmly by the loose tire. The train was traveling between Baltimore and Washington at nearly 70 miles and hour when the tire came loose.

A FROZEN MAIN AXLE BOX caused this Pennsylvania Railroad freight locomotive to derail and plunge into the river at Cedar Point, Pa.

THIS OLD ENGINE of the Milwaukee Road lost her leading truck after a derailment caused by a loose driver wheel tire. The accident happened in 1921 at Whitewater, Wis.

A DEFECTIVE LEADING WHEEL threw this Pennsy locomotive into a New Jersey sand bank, killing the fireman.

THIRTEEN CARS of a Boston & Albany passenger train were derailed by a broken wheel near Westfield, Mass., in November of 1939.

THE CENTER OF THE MAIN DRIVING WHEEL fragmented on a
B & O Baldwin ten-wheeler near Everitt, Ohio, in 1917. A detail
of the 1312's broken wheel clearly shows the fractured cast-iron
spokes and rim.

135

EIGHT PASSENGER COACHES of the Pennsy's *Pennsylvania Ltd.* rolled down an embankment at Warrior's Ridge, Pa., in February, 1912 after a broken arch bar on the tender spread the rails. The train uncoupled behind the first postal car and the front part of the train remained on the rails.

THE WRECK OF THE ILLINOIS CENTRAL'S *DIAMOND SPECIAL* near Springfield, Ill., in 1908. A broken wheel sent this old engine off the rails and down a steep embankment, to the delight of many young boys.

A COSTLY DERAILMENT on the Apache Railway near Snowflake Ariz., Feb. 3, 1947, was caused by a faulty journal on the tender. The locomotive overturned, crushing the cab and breaking off the steam pipes inside which filled the area with live steam. Two crew members trapped inside were scalded to death.

A PENNSY MOUNTAIN TYPE ENGINE broke a side rod. One end of the rod can be seen hanging down from the second wheel. The white "T" shaped area shows the fatigued part of the rod that caused the break. A crewman was injured in the accident.

THE WORST HOTBOX ACCIDENT in American railroad history struck the Pennsylvania Railroad's crack *Congressional Ltd.* at Frankfort, Pa., on Sept. 7, 1943. Eighty passengers died in the smash. This car was slashed open when it was hurtled against a signal bridge.

A BROKEN WHEEL caused this costly derailment of a Union Pacific freight near Fallon, Calif. in 1950. Bruised and maimed box cars and tank cars lie crazily across the tracks. From the belly of one punctured automobile carrier protrudes a shiny, but crumpled, new Lincoln.

NO EXIT: A brick wall did not stop this runaway. She burst through her roundhouse berth in Hartford, Conn. on July 8, 1905, narrowly missing a plunge into the river.

Honiss Oyster House, Hartford

Chapter Eleven

Runaways

IT SEEMS INCREDIBLE TODAY that railroads had reached mid-Victorian times and yet the locomotives themselves had no brakes at all. The only way to stop a moving train in most cases was by throwing the engine in reverse and by setting the hand brakes on the cars. Here was a major element of disaster which reoccurred again and again during nineteenth century railroad history. Trains needed a safe and sure method of stopping from the very beginning, but it took forty years before a satisfactory brake was devised. Not until George Westinghouse's airbrake of 1869 did there exist a dependable train brake.

There were no driving wheel brakes on locomotives before 1875, because wheel brakes were considered unnecessary. Some early locomotives had brakes operated by steam pressure, but many of the high wheeled passenger engines built as late as 1880 could not be stopped suddenly. If an engineer wanted to slow his train down, he would blow his whistle, and brakemen would scramble from car to car, setting the clumsy hand brakes. These early hand brakes were sometimes quite primitive, being much like stagecoach brakes: wooden blocks operated by a lever pressed against the wheels.

In a danger the time lag in this communication from engineer to brakeman could lead to ruin. If the brakeman did not set the brakes instantly, there could result collision or derailment. What was worse, if the brakemen could see that the train could not be stopped in time before an accident, they were likely to jump off in panic rather than remain at their posts. The train would then run away with the passengers trapped helpless inside.

The earliest cause of a runaway caused by faulty handbraking resulted in a collision between a train and a steamboat. The accident occurred on September 11, 1839, on the Camden & Amboy, which seems to have had more than its share of mishaps. On Wednesday noon a "most painful accident" occurred at the road's Amboy terminal steamboat landing. Here the tracks terminated in an inclined plane that lead the cars down to the river's edge and the boat docks on New York Bay, where the passengers would continue their journey to New York via steamer. The locomotive was detached, and the eight passenger cars containing over a hundred people were lowered down the grade to the wharf, their momentum held back by handbrakes on the cars. As the train

WHEN THE BRAKES FAILED, this Western Pacific engine splintered a standing caboose. The accident happened at Silver Zone, Nev. in the spring of 1936.

began down, it gathered speed. The brakeman tried to stop the runaway, but his brake was defective. Then he sprang to another car to use that brake, but by that time it was too late to stop the collision. The train sped down toward the pier.

The train crashed violently into the steamboat *Commerce,* which was lying there to receive passengers. The two forward cars were demolished, and the wheelhouse of the ship was "stove in and demolished." Luckily only a dozen people were injured. None was reported

killed. Since the tracks down to the wharf were in an inclined plane and since there was only one brakeman put on an eight-car train, we can only hold the railroad as operating irresponsibly. In the era of primitive braking it seems a folly to assume that a single man could safely control a multi-car train on a steep grade.

Scores of inventions and hundreds of patents sought a device to control and stop the momentum of the railroad train during the 1840's and 1850's. One ingenius system was the Loughridge Chain Brake designed in 1855. With this contrivance the brake shoe was applied to the rim of the wheel by winding a strong chain extending under the whole train and connecting with all the brakes. Another device was the steam brake, designed in 1848 by George Griggs, Master Mechanic of the Boston & Providence Railroad. Although the brake worked well enough, it was abandoned after a year because of a boiler explosion, which people believed was caused by the steam brake. There were others—spring brakes, hydraulic brakes, compressed air brakes—all attempts to find some substitute for hand brakes. None was really satisfactory though until the appearance of George Westinghouse's air brake. Westinghouse patented his brake in 1869, and it proved a dramatic success. The air brake al-

THIS B & O LOCOMOTIVE went on a runaway rampage in the middle of Chillicothe, Ohio, tearing up a couple of new engines and several freight cars.

lowed the engineer from his cab to set brakes mechanically throughout the whole train.

Strangely enough, the railroads were not interested in the Westinghouse brake. The redoubtable Commodore Vanderbilt's reply to Westinghouse was, "Do you pretend to tell me that you could stop trains with wind? I'll give you to understand, young man, that I am too busy to have any time taken up in talking to a damned fool." Rebuffed by railroad executives, Westinghouse travelled widely and proselytized endlessly on the subject of railroad safety. Not till 1886, when Iowa passed legislation requiring all trains in the state to use air brakes, was his brake seriously considered by the industry. Then in 1893 the Federal Government enacted the Railroads' Safety Appliance Act, which meant that all trains should be equipped with air brakes. By the turn of the century the air brake was standard on most main-line trains.

In railroad lore a "runaway" is the coasting or running out of control of a train. Sometimes runaways occur from brake failure and other times because the train crew failed to set their hand brakes. If, for instance, the crew didn't set enough hand brakes when the train stopped, a barely noticeable grade just might be enough to start the train rolling. In mountainous country the train could career down the tracks for miles, whizzing wildly around

curves and along rugged gorges. Railroad folklore is rich with such runaway stories, and the movies too have quite naturally capitalized on their romantic qualities.

The only major passenger train disaster caused by a runaway happened in the California Rockies at Tehachapi Summit. There on January 19, 1883, a Southern Pacific express, standing at rest on a steep mountain grade, slipped its brakes and began to roll backward. The seven cars (mail, express, baggage, two sleepers, coach, and smoker) slipped away by themselves. The two engines had been detached temporarily.

Rolling down the mountain, the train quickly gathered momentum and soon disappeared in the thin morning light. Careening down from Tehachapi Summit, 3549 feet high, the helpless train swept wickedly around a sharp curve after four miles and jumped the track at about seventy miles per hour, crashing over a deep ditch. The wreckage, piled in a frightful heap, quickly caught fire. Fifteen passengers died in the carnage. Among the dead were Mrs. John Downy, wife of the ex-governor of California, and ex-congressman Charles Larrabee of Wisconsin.

The cause of the accident was the crew's neglecting to set the brakes on the stopped train. The company tried to explain the care-

lessness by suggesting that a gang of thieves had deliberately released the brakes to allow the train to roll back to a spot where they could rob the train unnoticed. Such a theory sounds quite unlikely.

Two serious runaway accidents have happened in Washington, D. C., both for the same reason: brake failure. The first runaway took place on the morning of August 17, 1887, when the B & O's Cincinnati, Chicago and St. Louis Express came into the Capital City out of control at sixty miles an hour. Speeding to make up lost time, the engineer found that the air brakes would not work as he approached the city limits. Quickly he signaled for hand brakes, but the brakemen were unable to get the train under control. Coming into a "Y", the train jumped the track and smashed into a signal house. The engine was dragged off and plunged into someone's garden, and steam from the bursting boiler streamed into a neighboring house, scalding several people inside. The signal building was smashed to splinters, and the forward car totally crushed.

The second Washington runaway was the terrific Union Station wreck of January 15, 1953. The Pennsylvania's sixteen-car *Federal Express,* heavily loaded with visitors to attend

Eisenhower's inauguration five days later, left Boston at 11 p.m. the day before for its 459 mile overnight run to the nation's capital. It seemed like only a routine trip, but but at 8:38 the next morning at Union Station in Washington the *Federal* brought massive destruction— as a runaway.

On the trip down, the *Federal* ground to a halt at Kingston Swamp in Rhode Island. Conductor Ralph Ward had noticed a few sharp jerks, and he knew brakes were sticking somewhere on the train. A rapid check revealed that the brakes on the rear cars were jammed by a stuck angle cock on the air brake system of the third car. Engineer Matta opened the valve, and the brakes released correctly. The train went on after the fifty-six minute delay. From then on the brakes worked fine.

At New Haven the routine changes were made: diesels came off, and a big electric locomotive was put on; and, of course, the crews were changed (word of the trouble with the air brake was not, however, passed along to the new crew).

Between New York and Baltimore, with stops at Philadelphia and Wilmington, the brakes worked perfectly. After Baltimore, the new engineer, Harry Brower, gave the big electric the gun. He barreled along through the Maryland countryside at eighty miles an hour. Then two miles outside of Washington Union Station he made his first brake application. The long train didn't slow. Brower next set the emergency brake, which should have jammed all brakes and brought the *Federal* to a jarring halt, but it didn't. The express was running away out of control only a mile and a half from the station.

Frantically, Brower began to sound raucous blasts from his horn as his train headed downgrade for the dead-end track at the station. Telegraph operator Harry Ball at a signal tower a mile from the station heard the repeated blasts and knew the *Federal* was out of control. He called ahead to the stationmaster's office with the news, "There's a runaway coming at you on track sixteen — get the hell out of there." The split second warning was barely time enough to clear waiting passengers, porters, and vendors out of the vaulted concourse. In a second there was a screeching noise and a terrible thundering roar as it hit. The big GG-I engine plowed across the concourse, smashed

through the stationmaster's office, and completely demolished the main newsstand. Just as it was about to crash through into the main waiting room, the floor of the concourse suddenly gave way. Like a dying animal the heavy behemoth fell into the basement baggage room. Two coaches followed the engine into the cavernous hole. The station clock stopped dead at 8:30 a.m., setting the exact time of this sensational runaway.

By a miracle no one was in the baggage room that morning. Although no one died, the injured totaled eighty-seven. Property damage was estimated at a million dollars. The direct cause of the accident was the closed angle cock on the third car, the same valve that had caused trouble in Rhode Island. In addition to the usual ICC investigation, the Senate Committee on Interstate and Foreign Commerce held a special hearing on the wreck. Although the possibility of sabotage was brought up, the theory was never substantiated. The faulty brake system remained the plain and simple cause of the runaway.

ANOTHER VIEW of the Tehachapi runaway.

FREIGHT CARS LIE PILED HIGH in a messy jumble after a brake failure.

WASHINGTON CITY was the scene of two of the most famous runaway accidents in railroad history. The first occurred on the morning of Aug. 17, 1887, when a Baltimore & Ohio passenger train entered the city out of control at sixty miles an hour. At a curve the train jumped the track, demolishing several buildings and wrecking a string of coaches.

THE WESTINGHOUSE ATMOSPHERIC BRAKE.

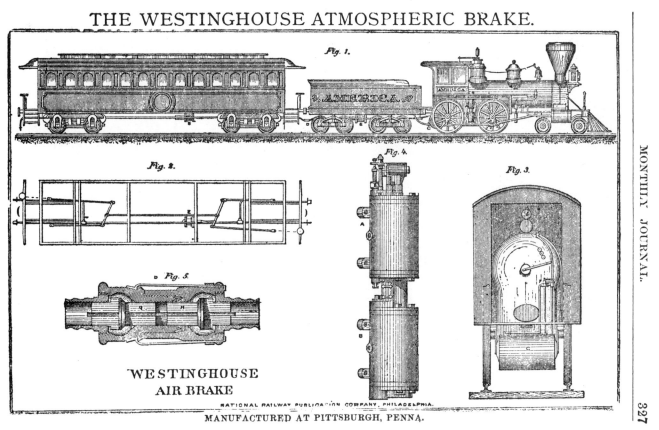

Fig. 1.

Fig. 2.   Fig. 4.   Fig. 3.

Fig. 5.

WESTINGHOUSE
AIR BRAKE

NATIONAL RAILWAY PUBLICATION COMPANY, PHILADELPHIA.

MANUFACTURED AT PITTSBURGH, PENNA.

A SERIOUS PILE-UP happened on the PRR at New Portage Jct., Pa., in 1916, killing seven employees. The brakes on a freight failed on a down mountain grade. The runaway collided with four engines at the foot of the mountain. ICC investigators blamed the engineer for allowing air brake pressure to become too low.

THE RESULT OF A RUNAWAY. A Wabash locomotive had her visage smashed and her cab totally crushed near Delray. Mich., on Feb. 23, 1925.

A LARGE CROWD gathered to look at the fractured remains of the Washington, D.C. runaway of 1887.

ANOTHER VIEW OF THE WASHINGTON RUNAWAY of 1887, with the Capitol dome in the background.

THE ALL-TIME SENSATIONAL RUNAWAY WRECK was the Washington, D.C. terminal disaster of 1953. Loaded with in-auguration-bound passengers, the Pennsy's crack *Federal Express* sped out of control headed straight for a dead end at the Capital's classical marble station. The express smashed through the station and into the main concourse where the floor collapsed under the weight. Luckily no one was killed.

Photo: Washington Evening Star

THE DANGER OF CROSSING COLLISIONS swelled rapidly with the popularity of the passenger car in the 1920's and 1930's. Signals such as this one were erected at many busy intersections to warn motorists.

Chapter Twelve

Crossing Accidents

Trains don't hit cows very often anymore. Locomotives don't even have cow-catchers. There was a time, though, when cows straying onto the tracks caused a good many accidents. Now, instead of cows, railroads face the danger of cars and trucks crossing the tracks in front of trains. Grade crossing accidents are today still a major cause of train wrecks. In 1960, 1,421 people were killed in such accidents.

Cowcatchers were one of the distinctive features of early American locomotives. European engines did not have these contrivances, which were also known as cattle guards or pilots. They were quite necessary in the States because of the hazard presented to trains by cattle wandering onto the tracks. It was many years before American lines could afford to fence their right-of-ways. Consequently stock from surrounding farms used the railway property as pastures. Collisions with cows, oxen, mules, hogs, and horses are common in the diaries of early rail travellers. The Ohio Railway Report for 1867 stated: "Cattle and other farm animals running at large and getting upon the track, is a constant source of annoyance and detention, and frequently serious accident." Also, incidentaly, railroads had to pay the owners of the animals they killed.

The purpose of the cowcatcher was to clear obstruction away from the train in order to prevent their getting under the wheels of the locomotive. If some bulky object got under one of these light engines, it was very often derailed. The Camden & Amboy Railroad was the very first to fit a cowcatcher to one of its engines. A man with the wonderful name of Issac Dripps is credited with installing such a device on the engine *John Bull* (now preserved in the Smithsonian Institute) in 1833. Soon the curious looking cowcatcher was put on other locomotives on the line. By the 1850's the rakish, V-shaped cowcatcher was so familiar that it gave American locomotives their distinctive silhouette. Today in the age of the diesel and fenced tracks the cowcatcher has quite disappeared.

There are some rather lively early accounts of train collisions with cows and mules. In 1846 an English gentleman by the name of Alexander Mackay kept these notes of his travels in the United States: "I left Baltimore by the late night train for Washington. For two-thirds of the way we went on smoothly enough, but then within ten miles

RAILROAD ACCIDENT NEAR CHICAGO.

THE WORST CROSSING ACCIDENT in early years happened in 1853 near Chicago when an express rammed an emigant train broadside, killing twenty-one.

of Washington, a violent jerk to the whole train appraised us that we had run against something. The engineer gradually slackened speed and on stopping we discovered that we had run against a cow which had been lying on the line. 'I can stand a hog but them cows are the devil to pay,' said the stoker as he proceeded with the help of some others to drag the carcass of the engine and deposit it on the side of the line.''

In another travel account called *Two Years on the Farm of Uncle Sam,* Charles Casey tells of a train trip he took in 1849: "On the West Chester line I remember once on looking ahead seeing three cows on the track about a hundred yards off. The driver sprung the whistle and immediately they commenced running straight on the line. Two were young and plunged sideways off and escaped, but the other we gained on fast, never slacking speed. Another moment and crunch, jolt, crunch and the poor creature lay a bruised and bleeding mass. I appealed to the conductor but he only observed that people should keep their cattle off the track. There

seems to be an intuitive fraternity between most of the animals and the engine. While the train stands, dogs run among the wheels and I have seen pigs come and luxuriate on the tar and grease that oozed from the wheel-boxes.''

Stalled or runaway wagons and carriages at grade crossings were another cause of disaster to trains. In most cases, streets in the cities and roads in the country had no protecting gates or watchmen. There was simply a large board put up on a post which said "Look Out For The Locomotive.'' In 1867 George Wright, Commissioner of Railways for Ohio, said that accidents at road crossings would continue so long as railroad companies fail to provide guards and warnings.

The need for an effective warning device at crossings prompted the State of Massachusetts to enact a law in 1835 requiring bells on all locomotives. One of the earliest operating rules of the Boston & Worcester Road charged enginemen to ring their bells at all road crossings at least eighty rods before they crossed. Other signal devices—whistles and headlights—were

THIS EARLY RAILROAD DISASTER was caused when a Camden and Amboy train hit Dr. Hannigan's surrey on Aug. 29, 1855, near Burlington, N.J. The good doctor was too deaf to hear the engineer's whistle as he approached the tracks. Twenty-three passengers died in the derailed cars.

put on early locomotives to warn travelers. Some credit William Norris with applying the first steam whistle to a locomotive; others say it was Thomas Rogers on the engine *Sandusky*, built in 1837. The headlight became necessary when night-time operation of trains became common about 1850. At first these headlamps burned kerosene; by the end of the century they were electrified.

Even the warning of whistles, bells, and headlamps failed always to prevent people from crossing the tracks in front of a train. An unfortunate accident occurred on the Boston & Worcester Road at Framington, Massachusetts in 1839. The stationmaster there reported: "I am grieved to say that our gravel train, in coming into the depot this forenoon, ran over Mr. Aaron Pratt, a worthy citizen of this village. Four of the cars passed over his body, and he was instantly killed. Mr. Pratt was seventy-five years old and very deaf. He did not

hear or notice the train until it was nearly upon him, and then in his effort to escape, he fell across the rail."

One early railroad disaster was caused by a train hitting a carriage at a crossing. On the morning of August 29, 1855, Dr. John T. Hannigan of Columbus, New Jersey, was on his way to make a call at Burlington not far from his home. As his surrey approached the crossing of the Camden & Amboy at the edge of town, the doctor failed to see the rear end of a train backing rapidly toward him. Neither did he notice the crossing guard, Mrs. Mary Cook, waving frantically to him. When about twenty feet from the train, Hannigan saw the cars and tried to stop his horses, but they panicked and dashed right in front of the train.

When the last car struck the team, one of the horses was caught underneath and derailed the last three cars. Twenty-three passengers died in one of the smashed cars. Oddly enough,

THE CAMDEN & AMBOY'S *JOHN BULL* was the first engine fitted with a cowcatcher in 1833. Isaac Dripps, master mechanic for the road, was the inventor.

Dr. Harrigan was unhurt. The engineer testified that he had blown his whistle repeatedly as he backed toward the crossing, but this warning couldn't have mattered very much. Dr. Hannigan was stone deaf.

The most bizarre crossing accident in the history of American railroading was a collision between a river schooner and a passenger train of the Hudson River Railroad in 1851. The engineer's own story is: "With a crash and slam my meditiations were interrupted, and the whole side of the cab with the smokestack, whistle-stand and sand box were stripped from the engine. The splinters flew around my head, the escaping steam made most an infernal din, and the firebox emitted most as infernal a smoke. Lo! and behold it was a Hudson River schooner with which I had collided. It had, during the fog, been blown upon the shore, and into its bowsprit, which projected over the track, I had run full tilt."

To most people the words "Grade crossing" refer to the intersection of a railroad track and a highway. There are also grade crossings consisting of two intersecting railroad lines. These are called "diamond" crossings in railroad jargon, no doubt because of the diamond shape formed by the intersecting tracks. "Diamond" crossings were always very dangerous, even when railroads were young and train speeds slow.

One of the worst examples of a crossing collision between two trains was the calamitous clash on the outskirts of Chicago at a place called Grand Crossing. The collision took place at ten o'clock in the evening of April 25 of the year the disasters began—1853. At the time it was the deadliest rail accident in American history.

An eastbound Michigan Central express, headed for Toledo, rammed a Michigan Southern emigrant train broadside, killing twenty-one German emigrants. According to an eye witness, the wrecked cars lay piled up in a swamp which flanked the tracks. The scene was: "An immense heap of iron, splinters, doors, and baggage with the crushed locomotive of the express train hissing steam from its ruptured boiler. Groans and cries assailed the ears of those who hastened from the first class cars. Time will not efface the memory of that terrible and heart-rending spectacle from the mind of the unwilling beholder. A heap of ruins, from beneath which shrieked out upon the midnight air cries for help, mingled in strong discord with the deeper groans of the dying."

Gross carelessness and ignorant rivalry between the crews of both trains caused the wreck. Evidence showed that Buckman, engineer of the Michigan Central train, could have avoided the collision either by stopping or going on, but as he had the right-of-way he took his time in passing through the intersection. His petty attitude of "me first" took twenty-one lives. Also, his train was running at night without a headlight.

Fortunately, there are few serious "diamond" collisions today. Companies have always recognized these crossings as especially dangerous and have made every attempt to avoid trains crossing at the same level.

Today the chief danger of accidents at railroad grade crossings is from motor vehicles. After 1860 when locomotives became heavier, the hazard caused by carriages and wagons was not very great; the horse carriages were light and of wood, and the locomotive was usually quite powerful enough to push it aside or crunch it to bits. The fifty-year immunity from highway crossing dangers began to diminish, however, with the advent of motor cars. By about the 1920's Americans took to their automobiles in great numbers. These early cars could easily cause derailment if they got under the wheels of the train.

The greatest source of highway crossing collisions today is clearly the truck. Hundreds of heavy gasoline and fuel oil tankers, flat bed trailers, bulldozers, cranes, and earth movers cross in front of trains every day. These heavily-weighted, slow-moving trucks can easily destroy a train. Although almost all highway crossings are now protected by automatic warning signals, motorists and truck drivers frequently disregard them and dash across, sometimes just ahead of a speeding train. One of the chief factors in truck-train collisions is carelessness of the truck drivers, who fail to observe safety signals. Truck-train collisions are now so numerous that a special division of the new Department of Transportation is set up to investigate them: the Motor Carrier Investigation Unit.

One deadly truck-train accident happened on March 1, 1960, when a Santa Fe passenger train hit a heavy tanker truck carrying 6,465 gallons of crude oil at Rosedale, California. The train was derailed by the impact, and the wreckage immediately ignited. Fourteen people lost their lives in the inferno.

On September 17, 1963, a make-shift bus loaded with fifty-eight migrant Mexican farm workers drove onto the Southern Pacific track in front of a fast moving freight at Chualar, California. Thirty-two passengers of the bus died, and all the rest were severely injured.

On October 15, 1966, a Chicago, Burlington & Quincy passenger train struck a dump truck carrying 30,000 lbs. of rock at a crossing near Island Park, Iowa. The train travelling at seventy-two miles per hour was mostly derailed, and the two diesel-electric locomotives were heavily damaged. Although the truck was completely destroyed, the driver was not killed. The accident was caused by the truck driver's failure to stop until the train had passed. Although it was a clear morning, the driver said he didn't notice the train coming.

HATTIE MESSERSMITH'S brand new Buick got demolished when she forgot to look both ways at a crossing.

A DIRECT HIT, broadside. This mangled schoolbus stalled on the B & O tracks near Rockville, Md. in 1959. Fortunately the bus was empty, and the driver was able to jump out just before the *Metropolitan* crashed into it at 70 mph.

A TRUCK-TRAIN COLLISION near Michigan City, Ind. sent this Chesapeake & Ohio locomotive spinning off the rails in 1963.

THIRTY-TWO MIGRANT FARM WORKERS died at Chualar, Calif. in 1963 when their makeshift bus was driven onto the tracks in front of a Southern Pacific freight. The driver was charged with manslaughter.

ANOTHER VIEW with the wreckage of the bus plastered to the front of the locomotive near Chualar, Calif.

ON OCT. 15, 1966, a Chicago, Burlington & Quincy passenger train truck a dump truck hauling stone near Island Park, Iowa. The diesel units were destroyed and the rest of the cars derailed.

THE TRUCK DRIVER caused the wreck at Island Park when he failed to stop to let the train go by. Although his truck was torn to pieces, the driver was not killed.

WITH HER FACE SCORCHED AND BATTERED, this Union Pacific passenger locomotive has just struck a gasoline tank truck at Rolla, Colo. The truck driver and train engineer and fireman were killed. The cause of this wreck on Nov. 20, 1965, was the trucker's failure to stop at the grade crossing.

JUST MINUTES AFTER THE ACCIDENT and before any changes had taken place, a local photographer snapped this shot near Shreveport, La. Although the explosion stopped the engine dead, the tender was thrown ahead, and the momentum of the freight cars crushed the engine's cab, killing the crew. The accident occurred on the Texas & Pacific road on Aug. 19, 1927.

Chapter Thirteen

Boiler Explosions

Locomotive boiler explosions have never been a great cause of serious railroad accidents or loss of life. Although boilers did explode with some frequency during the days of steam, fewer passengers were killed than in other kinds of accidents, such as collisions and derailments. In 1875, for example, there were 1,201 railroad accidents reported in this country. Only twenty-nine of that total were boiler explosions; there were by contrast 278 collisions that year. Fifty years later in 1925 the number of boiler explosions remained the same—twenty-nine, out of a total list of accidents numbering 20,785. Although boiler explosions rarely killed passengers, they were in nearly all cases deadly for the engineer and firemen in the cab.

As stated in Chapter 2, the first railroad fatality in America resulted from the boiler which burst on the South Carolina Railroad's *Best Friend of Charleston* in 1831, killing the fireman. After the explosion of the *Best Friend* passengers on the line were protected from a recurrence of the accident by a "barrier car" piled high with bales of cotton. (see Chapter 1). This "barrier car" was placed between the locomotive and the cars to protect passengers from steam and flying metal should the boiler burst.

Another early boiler explosion took place in Union Square in New York City on the Fourth of July, 1839. A locomotive on the Harlem Road was hauling a big holiday crowd downtown to the depot near City Hall when it ran off the track in the middle of Union Square. A crowd soon gathered around the hissing machine, enjoying the fun of seeing the spectacle. Ordinarily, the derailment would have caused no problem. Unfortunately, however, the engine crew was so busy trying to get the engine back on the track that they forgot to watch the steam gauge. Pressure built up while they were at work, and the boiler burst open with a terrific roar. According to a bystander, "The chief engineer was blown to pieces. His legs went into Union Park, his arms to a pile of lumber on the other side of the avenue, and his head was split in two parts. His abdomen was also burst, and his intestines scattered over the road." A brakeman was also killed, and five onlookers were severely injured.

On March 18, 1912, there was a thunderous explosion at the shops of the Southern Pacific Railroad at San Antonio, Texas. A locomotive had just received heavy repairs, and steam pressure was being raised in the boiler before putting the engine back in service. As an employee was setting the safety valves, the boiler blew up. The explosion completely destroyed the locomotive and badly damaged the surrounding buildings. One chunk of the boiler weighing 16,000 pounds was blown about 1,200 feet. Another part weighing about 900 pounds flew 2,250 feet, ripping the side out of a frame house. In all twenty-six people were killed and thirty-two injured in the explosion.

A large portion of boiler explosions in locomotives are the result of what is called a crown sheet failure—or overheating of the crown sheet due to low water. When the water level inside the boiler runs to low, the fire attacks the metal directly and heats it red-hot. If, then, water runs in suddenly on the intensely heated crown sheet surface, a development of steam takes place instantly, and an explosion results.

Such an explosion can only happen through neglect on the part of the locomotive crew, as water gauges indicate the height of the water in the boiler.

Sometimes boiler explosions were so great that the entire boiler on the locomotive was blown some distance. An example of this damage occurred near Powellton, West Virginia, on December 27, 1934. The locomotive, owned and operated by the Elkhorn Piney Coal Company, was attached to a labor train on the mining company's property. The force of the explosion hurled the boiler fifty feet into the air and crashing into a wooden passenger car. The car was horribly crushed by the impact of the heavy boiler. Seventeen persons, all employees of the coal mining company, were killed. Forty--three were badly hurt.

A RARE BOILER FAILURE (explosion of the front course) is shown in this view of an old Baldwin eight wheeler on the Houston & Texas Central Railroad.

THESE SOUTHERN PACIFIC accident investigators take time away from their duties to pose for a photograph amid the debris from a boiler explosion. At their rear a wrecking train has arrived. In the close up view the powerful wreck crane tugs to place the boiler on a flat car for return to the shops. The explosion occurred on April 4, 1912.

ALTHOUGH THE BOILER AND CAB WERE BLASTED CLEAN AWAY in the explosion, this "Katy" mogul remained on the rails. In fact, she rolled on for fifty-five feet beyond the point of the explosion. The scene is Cumby, Texas, 1921.

THE TEXAS & NEW ORLEANS RAILROAD lost their Vauclain Compound in the drought of 1913. The exploding boiler threw the engine and train off the rails near Houston, Texas.

HEAVING CRAZILY after a crown sheet explosion, this Rock Island locomotive presents an odd contrast to the symmetrical regularity of row on row of wheels in the Pratt, Kansas yards. The force of the explosion thrust the engine up and onto her sister, where she rested for a moment before crashing to the ground. The accident happened Dec. 11, 1919.

THE ENTRAILS OF A SANTA FE LOCOMOTIVE lie bent and gnarled after a violent disembowelment near Standish, Mo. in the winter of 1921.

THE THUNDEROUS BLAST of a bursting locomotive boiler announced disaster over the countryside. Connecticut farmers who gathered quickly about this wreck stare curiously at the iron beast with her belly ripped open.

A GRIM GENT points to the fatal flaw shortly after a SP locomotive shattered her boiler at the round-house at Hondo, Tex., in 1912. In another view the townsfolk gather round to inspect the remains.

DESTRUCTION OF
C.M. ST.R ROUNDHOUSE

MITCHELL
S.D.
SEPT. 5
1916

THE MILWAUKEE ROAD lost a roundhouse and the service of several engines in a shattering explosion at Mitchell, S. D., in the fall of 1916.

PERHAPS ONE OF THE MOST SERIOUS CATASTROPHES resulting from the explosion of a locomotive boiler was at San Antonio, Texas, on March 18, 1912. On that day a locomotive that was undergoing repair in the Southern Pacific shops exploded with a terrific force. The explosion completely destroyed the locomotive and many of the surrounding buildings. One great chunk of the boiler weighing 16,000 pounds was blown about 1,200 feet. Other pieces shattered dwellings and stores. In all twenty-six people were killed in the blast.

A CROWN SHEET FAILURE plopped this St. Louis Southwestern's boiler neatly beside the engine at Paragould, Ark. in 1945.

THE NEW YORK CENTRAL'S 5839 lies rotting in the snow near Starbrick, Pa. after a crown sheet failure.

TWO DAYS AFTER CHRISTMAS 1934 a car load of miners and their families were returning to their homes and jobs on the company-owned railroad of the Elkhorn Piney Coal Mining Company. Without any warning the locomotive's boiler burst violently, hurled into the air, and fell heavily into the first wooden coach, squashing it like an egg. Seventeen people inside were crushed to death, and forty-three were badly injured in this accident, which happened near Powellton, W. Va.

EYELESS IN GAZA: A Chicago & Eastern Illinois Mikado tipped off a single line track near Pimento, Ind., on Aug. 15, 1936, after the boiler burst open.

THE NORFOLK & WESTERN lost a brand new Mallet on July 7, 1942. When the big engine was involved in a collision at Nolan, W. Va., the boiler exploded, vaulting some two hundred feet off the track to crush a farmer's prize Buick.

IN A ROCKY CUT near Lehigh, Pa., a double-headed Lackawanna passenger train blew up on a steep grade in late July 1930. The twisted fire box and boiler of the 1172 were thrown fifty yards ahead.

THE NEW YORK CENTRAL'S light Pacific 3361 lost her boiler at Bergen, N.Y., in July 1928.

THE SERENITY OF THE FARMLANDS around Casper, Calif., was shattered on the morning of May 3, 1941. The boiler of a big Southern Pacifc freight burst apart, scattering shrapnel into fields and dwellings. By mid-morning throngs appeared to gaze at the ruined farmhouse. A great chunk of the boiler lies in the field across the road, already covered with a tarpaulin, pending ICC investigation.

THE LETOHATCHIE, ALA., water tower looms ominously behind a ruined L & N locomotive: a reminder of the peril of low water in the boiler. The engine, which had been hauling a freight train, stopped on Jan. 3, 1944, to take on needed water. Before the crew had time to fill the tank, the crownsheet blew. The force of the explosion ripped the boiler from the frame and sent it somersaulting into a concrete overpass 116 feet ahead.

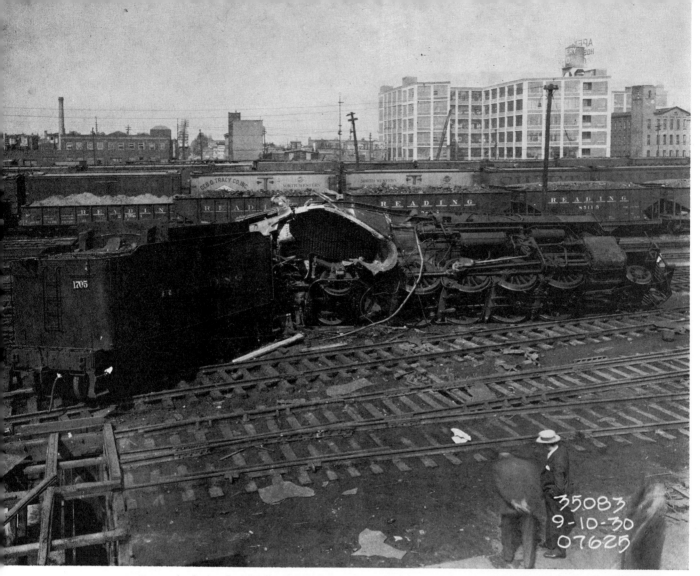

LOW WATER in the boiler flopped this Reading Company Mikado on her side in the Philadelphia yards on a bright fall day in 1930. The detailed view shows how the crown sheet pulled entirely loose from the stay bolts of the engine.

AN EXPLOSION on the New York, New Haven & Hartford, Dec. 19, 1890, at Wallingford, Conn. The sandbox shot off the top of the boiler, sailed high in the air, and crashed down through the roof of a nearby house. Somehow the crew escaped with their lives.

LOOKING LIKE FROZEN SPAGHETTI STRANDS, these superheater tubes lie exposed after Southern Pacific No. 4402 burst near Richvale, Calif. on Christmas Day, 1931.

READY FOR SCRAPPING: The tremendous impact of explosion crunched and creased one-inch thick boiler plates and tubes of the New York Central's 2758.

Selected Bibliography

Adams, Charles Francis. *Notes on Railroad Accidents.* New York: Putnams, 1879.

The American Railway. New York: Scribners, 1897.

Burford, Cary Clive. *The Chatsworth Wreck.* Fairbury, Ill.: Blade Publ., 1949.

Dunbar, Seymour. *A History of Travel in America.* Indianapolis: Bobs-Merrill, 1946.

Fagan, J. O. *Confessions of a Railroad Signalman.* New York: Houghton Mifflin, 1908.

Grayland, Eugene C. *There Was Danger on the Line.* Auckland, New Zealand: Belvedere, 1954.

Hamilton, James A. B. *British Railway Accidents of the Twentieth Century.* London: Unwin, 1967.

Howland, S. A. *Steamboat Disasters and Railroad Accidents in the United States.* Worcester: Dorr, 1846.

Keir, Malcolm. *The March of Commerce,* Vol 4 of *The Pageant of America.* New Haven: Yale Un. Press, 1927.

Larimer, J. McCormick. Bucyrus: *The Railroad Wrecker.* Muskogee, Okla.: Muskogee, 1909.

Mencken, August. *The Railroad Passenger Car.* Baltimore: Johns Hopkins, 1957.

Meredith, Matt. J. *First Anniversary of the Mud Run Disaster.* Pittsburgh: Oliver, 1889.

Nock, Oswald S. *Historic Railway Disasters.* London: Allan, 1966.

Peet, Stephen D. *The Ashtabula Disaster.* Chicago: Goodman, 1877.

Rolt, Lionel T. *Red for Danger.* London: Bodley Head, 1955.

Shaw, Robert B. *Down Brakes.* London, Macmillan, 1961.

Stover, John F. *American Railroads.* Chicago: Chicago Un. Press, 1961.

Trips in the Life of a Locomotive Engineer. New York: Bradburn, 1863.

With, Emile. *Railroad Accidents.* Boston: Little Brown, 1856.

ARTIFICIAL LIMBS

CRIPPLES RESTORED TO THEIR USEFULNESS

——BY THE USE OF——

Artificial Limbs with India-Rubber Hands and Feet

(MARKS' PATENTS.)

Over thirty years' experience in the treatment of every class of amputation, deformity or deficiency, with unequaled success; has gained the confidence of the profession and popularity among the crippled. The rubber hands and feet dispense with complicated articulations, and afford every requisite movement for good, natural, easy and graceful use of the member, with vastly increased durability. Men with both their legs artificial are enabled to attend their vocations without detection. Arms restore the appearance and assist greatly in the performance of labor.

Illustrated pamphlet of 150 pages, containing valuable information, sent FREE to those giving satisfactory description of their cases. U. S. Government Manufacturer. Surgeons, as well as disabled soldiers and mutilated persons, should have a copy of the pamphlet. We desire to call *special attention* of railroad officials who are purchasing artificial limbs for their employees. The simplicity of these limbs render them of special importance to railroad men.

Invalid and Rolling Chairs and Crutches to meet any demand.

A. A. MARKS, 691 Broadway, New York.

EARLY TIME TABLES featured speed and safety and sometimes when space was left over canned goods!

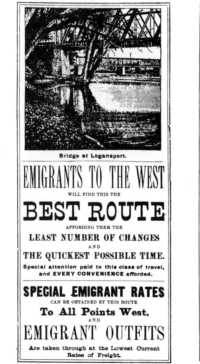

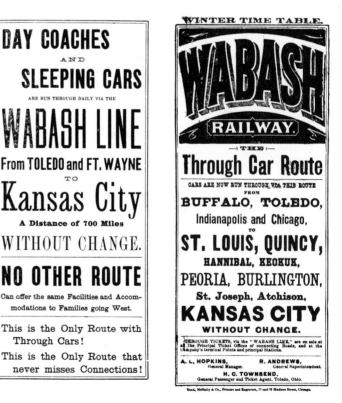